THE FORMATION OF SOCIAL POLICY
IN THE
CATHOLIC AND JEWISH TRADITIONS

The Formation of Social Policy in the Catholic and Jewish Traditions

EUGENE J. FISHER and
DANIEL F. POLISH, editors

UNIVERSITY OF NOTRE DAME PRESS
Notre Dame, Indiana 46556

Library of Congress Cataloging in Publication Data

Main entry under title:

The Formation of social policy in the Catholic and
  Jewish traditions.

  1. United States—Social policy. 2. Church and social problems—
Catholic Church. 3. Judaism and social problems.   I. Fisher,
Eugene J.   II. Polish, Daniel F.
HN65.F67   261.8'3   80-50268
ISBN 0-268-00953-8
ISBN 0-268-00951-1 (pbk.)

Manufactured in the United States of America

Contents

7029489

Introduction

THE GREATEST THREAT TO religious faith may not be disbelief but the irrelevance of religious belief in the life of the believer. It is not simply that "religious" people have done terrible things to one another in the name of religion. Nor is it a question of the sublime paradox posed by Dostoevsky in "The Grand Inquisitor," that people are capable of committing "irreligious," even sacrilegious, acts to preserve religious institutions. The deeper problem is that numbers of nominally religious people can commit unethical acts, of greater or smaller magnitude, without reference to the values or moral instruction of their religious traditions. Guards at the death camps of Nazi Europe, in many instances, continued to participate in the rites of their churches. Thieves, swindlers, cheats, miscreants on grand scale and small often consider themselves to be religious people and seem unperturbed by the difference between their actions and the standards of their professed faith.

To the credit of organized religious life in America, the disengagement of belief from action has not characterized the mandate or the activities of the various communities of faith. Religious leaders have consistently addressed themselves to the moral aspects of the internal affairs of their respective bodies, as well as to local issues, national and international affairs. For good or ill, religious involvement is credited with shaping American society's attitude on such major questions as the teaching of evolution in public schools, prohibition, the struggle for civil rights, the Vietnam War. Indeed in the late 50s and through the 60s it appeared as if religious leadership was the crucial catalyst in the movement for social change.

Of late, there has been considerable retrenchment in social activism in general in the country. American society as a whole has moved toward privatization and political quiescence. Reflecting this step, local religious leaders have tended to shift their activity from social action to social service, to emphasize the perhaps unduly neglected dimension of inwardness and the spiritual quest.* Despite this shift in priorities, the national bodies of the various religious communities continue to involve themselves in the issues confronting American society. At recent count there were no less than thirty-eight offices of religious groups in Washington devoted to matters of social policy. Representatives of Protestant, Catholic, and Jewish bodies can be found addressing themselves to the whole lexicon of concerns from abortion to Zimbabwe/Rhodesia with all the stops in between: boat people, criminal code reform, drug abuse, euthanasia, full employment, gun control, terrorism, undocumented aliens, voter registration, welfare reform, etc.

While it is correct and even healthy that religious people and religious institutions should involve themselves in the problems of society, increasingly there has been a concern about the stance from which these involvements are pur-

---

*Clearly, the two voices, the social and the spiritual, need not speak one at the expense of the other. Both are essential aspects of authentic religiosity. Indeed, it can be argued that each leads to the other, since both stand, at root, for commitment to the ideal of transcendence of self and self-interest.

sued. We do not refer here to the argument that religion should not involve itself in the affairs of the world. Those of us who have been engaged in such matters are familiar enough with the expressions of shocked indignation from those who find themselves on the other side of some issue: "Religion should not meddle in such matters. Go back to teaching morality." As often as not, the indignation is feigned, and we are liable to encounter the former adversaries, who were concerned that religion not "sully itself in political quagmires," at our door imploring us to involve ourselves on their side of some other issue.

Nor need we concern ourselves here with the matter of representativeness of religious statements. Elected officials are wont to ask "Where are your troops?" However sincere its intent, the question seems more reminiscent of Stalin's query about the Pope, asked out of derision rather than naive curiousity: "How many divisions does he have?" The case can be made, it seems to us, that religious representatives do not necessarily serve the role of elected officials, as most narrowly understood. They do not have to speak representatively for their constituents. Indeed, they are as likely speaking *to* their membership as *for* them, and certainly should be not understood as expressing the sentiments of all of them.

The question we want to pose is the deeper one, not expressed by opponents of positions that may have been taken nor by elected officials to whom such positions were represented. The deeper question is the one we must pose to ourselves: by what authority do we speak? If our task is not alone to articulate the opinions of the membership of our respective communities, how do we go about framing our position? In what authenticity do we address social issues?

Religious institutions have been depicted, derided, and, we believe, caricatured, as responding reflexively to the ideologies of respective nonreligious forces (big labor, big business, the ADA, or the Chamber of Commerce). Ideally, religious positions are not framed in doctrinaire response to some external ideology, any more than by keeping an ear to the ground, a finger to the wind, or a hand on the pulse of public opinion. Ideally, religious stances on matters of social concern emerge from the encounter of the ethical teaching of a community with a specific issue.

It was in response to a sense that this ideal warranted reassertion and reaffirmation that the Synagogue Council of America and the United States Conference of Catholic Bishops convened a symposium on the subject of religious bases of social policy in the spring of 1979. Believing that more light could be shed on this central subject by joint exploration than by separate introspections, Jewish and Catholic social thinkers and activists sat together to probe the core of their own, and one another's, social policy.

In the process of those discussions, of which this book is a distillate, it became clear that significant factors make the ideal easier to delineate than to attain. In the first place, the ideal suggests that it is possible for there to be direct encounter between tradition and objective realities. The harsh truth is that the encounter of inherited tradition with current social problems is mediated through informed individuals, the organized entities they serve, and the institutional processes of those bodies.

The individuals are themselves not *tabulae rasae*. In addition to their relatedness to their religious traditions, they are men and women of the world, shaped by the various intellectual currents of that world, with sympathies and perspectives not wholly the products of their religious commitments. To some extent these "external" considerations do shape the way they perceive or transmit the tradition's values. Even the individual proclivities and ideosyncratic angles of vision with which each of us, as unique creatures, are endowed, will affect the way our tradition is refracted through us. This is so despite our efforts to strive for full fidelity to inherited wisdom.

The bodies that speak to and for the various religious communities are not themselves free of institutional considerations. Thus, a given position on a particular subject may be perceived as inimical to the welfare of the community which the agency represents. Or it may be seen as threatening or enhancing the leadership role of the representative body itself, within its community, or within the broader society. No doubt a given agency will be responsive to concerns of historical alliances or coalitions in which it participates. Such considerations of collective welfare or even institutional self-interest inevitably affect the way in which issues are chosen for consideration, and they play some role in determining what is said about them.

The decision-making process of a particular organization may have an effect on the way issues are addressed and discussed. It may inform the way in which positions are articulated and enacted. This systemic factor is not of a piece with the simple reflection of a tradition's response to a given issue. It is the clothing such a response wears. But it cannot help but contribute to the way the response is perceived.

The intrusion of extratraditional considerations in the process of formulating a position expressive of the tradition raises the question of whether it is, in today's fragmented reality, possible to articulate a distinctively religious position as opposed to one which merely echoes one of the ethical-humanistic positions which are represented in the intellectual and political marketplaces of ideas.

The simple application of traditional values to contemporary issues in the process of making social policy is rendered even more problematic by the very complexity of issues which are addressed. While the discipline of ethics enjoys the seeming luxury of delineating good from evil, social policy is most often in the position of weighing relative goods. At times, positive values, each endorsed by traditions, are found to be in conflict with one another. The simple appeal to tradition cannot rescue framers of religious social policy from this dilemma, for they are often placed in the difficult position of having to compromise tradition's absolute values for the sake of obtaining a relative improvement of conditions.

Another complicating factor is that which can be called the problem of contingent issues. Often the evil of an objective situation is clear and can be condemned in consonance with tradition. The goal to be attained may be equally apparent and no less endorsed by the teachings of one's community of faith. But the path from problem to resolution is not clearly delineated at all. The tradition provides little guidance about means. And, with some frequency, it is precisely over choice of means of remedy that issues are fought in the arena of political reality in which articulators of social policy contend. While the ethical tradition can be looked to to identify the ultimate goal, its voice is muted in the difficult choice among possible paths to this desired end. Pope John Paul II, while still a cardinal, noted that when religion must address complex, contingent political questions, it should do so "without lamentation, without exhortation, and without moralizing." In the course of the colloquium, both Bryan Hehir and Michael Wyschogrod suggested that the dilemma of contingent ethics devolves itself fundamentally to the fact that it is easier to identify what never should be done, what is abnormal evil, than to decide responsibly among the alternative courses of what might be done. Traditional teaching provides woeful little help in identifying which "should" is the best route to the "ought."

Yet another factor which complicates the idea picture evolved earlier is that of stance. As John Pawlikowski notes, there are times when a proper social policy voice is that of a prophet, denouncing evil, decrying and condemning it, though not actively working to right it. Other times call for the revolutionary, who upends the status quo root and branch to eliminate the evil in it. At some moments we are called to be social reformers, ameliorating symptoms without necessarily solving the fundamental problems that gave rise to them. And some circumstances call us to be healers who restore the rent fabric of society, giving it equilibrium in its dislocation. Religious teachings of various traditions recognize all these roles but do not necessarily tell us when each is most appropriate or when to assume which stance.

These are not questions which are put forward by those who oppose religious involvement in social issues. Rather they demand the serious attention of the very religious representatives who engage in such activity. The fundamental question is less "who speaks for the church" than "with what authenticity do I represent my tradition's teaching on this subject?"

The fundamental question to which this book is addressed is that of the methodology which is employed by Jewish and Catholic groups as they articulate policy on social issues. The form of the presentation is a parallel discussion of the methodological concerns in representative questions from three broad areas: family matters, domestic issues, and international affairs. A preliminary section is directed to the respective social structures of the Jewish and Catholic communities. A concluding section seeks to articulate the broad patterns of methodology that emerge from all of the representative issues as they are addressed in each community. This last section attempts also to draw comparisons between the methodological process of Catholics and Jews.

One factor seems clear to us. Two *distinct* forms of argument are represented in the papers. Jews and

Catholics manifest different styles of formulating their thoughts about social issues. Each has its obvious strengths, and it is not suggested that one is superior to the other. The difference is inescapably and clearly exemplified in this collection. The Catholic papers involve an explication of theological underpinnings, a clear discussion of the development of the theoretical structure which frames consideration of the moral decisions that are made. There is rich ratiocination and rigorous logic reflected in them. The Jewish papers are, in the main, less theologically explicated. They are formulated less analytically. Instead, they express an emotional intensity, a passion to take the prophetic statement and make it live in the immediate situation. What further generalizations can be made, and what their implications, these must be left to further discussion.

The goal of this endeavor has been to hold up the norm of faithful expression of the tradition as the ideal to be aspired to in religious response to social issues, even in the face of the complex factors which make this difficult. It is our hope that in presenting this colloquium we have called attention to the need for theological authenticity in the religious discussion of social policy. And we express the prayerful hope that we have furthered Jewish-Catholic respect and understanding as together we look forward to, and work for, the day when

> Faithfulness and truth meet
> Justice and well-being kiss
> Truth springs up from the earth
> Justice looks down from Heaven
> (Psalm 85)

D.F.P.

I. The Social Policy-Making Structures of our Religious Communities

Introduction

THESE INITIAL PAPERS BY two religious leaders, both veterans in the field, are descriptions of the way in which the organized religious communities they represent proceed in determining their social policies.

The two communities are manifestly different in structure. The Church, though opening up since the Second Vatican Council through application of the principle of collegiality, is a hierarchy. Its official spokespersons are clearly and canonically defined. The Jewish community is diverse and decentralized, with numerous groups representing varying perspectives.[1] Since actual membership often overlaps, Rabbi Balfour Brickner's description is especially helpful in summarizing the rich complexity of Jewish organizational life.

Each of the patterns of structuring, Catholic and Jewish, has advantages and disadvantages from religious as well as pragmatic perspectives. Each is susceptible to criticism and change from within. On the Jewish side, for example, the proliferation of organizations allows access to the process by a wide group of individuals. But, as Rabbi Brickner points out, one problem in the Jewish community today may be "too much spokespersonship and not enough leadership."

On the Catholic side, the National Conference of Bishops is a new juridical reality within the Church, with its nature and functioning still developing. The U.S. was one of the few countries in the world to have such a conference prior to the Second Vatican Council, and it is still working out its own role based on the Council's deliberations. Catholics, as Msgr. George Higgins has noted, are still working "to implement the corollaries of our renewed ecclesiology in the realm of public policy." Msgr. Francis Lally's paper outlines in concrete fashion the procedure which the Conference employs in developing a policy statement.

NOTE

1. "Religious vs. secular" is frequently cited as a primary distinction in perspective within the Jewish community. The distinction, though helpful, needs to be applied with caution, especially by Catholics, who understand the terms somewhat differently within the context of their own tradition.

Social Policy-Making Structures of the Jewish Community

BALFOUR BRICKNER

IT SEEMS TO ME THAT the key words in this title are "social policy." "Social policy," as I define it for the purposes of this presentation, has to do with the expressed attitude of a community on matters affecting social relationships. Moreover, "social *policy*" implies advocacy as well as opinion. One may have an attitude or an opinion without any action involved. However, the moment the concept of a policy is introduced, action—that is to say, taking or advocating a course of behavior—seems to be implied. What is being asked then in the question posed by this title is really: How does the Jewish community determine what it wants to *do* or say publicly on a whole host of socially significant issues such as church-state separation, freedom of choice in abortion, equal rights for women, civil rights for homosexuals, an energy policy for America, whether or not to reduce if not eliminate nuclear armaments? Beyond this, the question suggests that those who ask it also want to know how the Jewish community arrives at the positions it takes. Thus, what is the process of the decision making?

It is not the purpose of this paper to describe those positions the Jewish community takes on any of these

issues or others unlisted. Neither shall I defend or criti-
cize particular policies, though on some I would dearly
love to do either or both. My task is only to describe *how*
the process for decision making operates and what the
structures are that enable that process. That is a sufficiently formidable assignment.

Jewish organizational spokespersons dislike making or
having made for or about them a distinction between
"lay" and "religious." They prefer instead to speak of
a Jewish people, who constitute, combine, and express
both a religious and an ethnic quality, both intertwined
in a peculiar amalgam known as "peoplehood." Distinctions between the secular and the religious are not only
false, they claim, but distort the true image of what is
a Jew.

Correct as this may be, in the area of structure and
process of social policy decision making, distinctions between the religious and the lay communities have to be
drawn, if for no other reason than to help one more
clearly understand the processes involved. Moreover,
there are important differences even within these distinct, if perhaps somewhat artificially bifurcated, communities. Finally, division of functions within organizational structures of communities of nonreligious institutions and agencies makes for different processes of decision making. Groups dealing with advocacy on domestic
policy matters function one way, while groups devoted
exclusively or primarily to fund raising for Israel function
in another and totally different fashion Agencies that
deal exclusively with family service come to their decisions in yet another way, while those whose primary interest is the promotion of Jewish culture or art arrive at
their policy decisions in yet a different fashion. Sometimes, as in the Jewish community's almost universal

support for the state of Israel, the views and policies of all the various agencies and groups coincide.

A seasoned Jewish professional eventually learns the intricacies of these convoluted and often intersecting paths. They learn how to consult, and, most of all, not to infringe on one another's "turfs." Sometimes however, organizational competition leads to confrontation and an occasional unpleasantness. Thus, one would not find the United Jewish Appeal or the Israel Bond Corporation or the Conference of Presidents of Major Jewish Organizations (three highly visible and, in the case of the first two, quite large, organizations) making policy statements or decisions on the Bakke case or ERA. Neither would you find the National Jewish Community Relations Council becoming involved in policy decisions affecting whether or not Jewish philanthropic dollars raised in this country for Israel ought to be spent there for specific religious institutions such as a yeshiva.

The Religious Community

How does the Jewish *religious* community determine its social policies? What are its structures and processes? We begin here, perhaps because we know that structure most intimately and perhaps because it is the least complicated to describe.

Basically there are three main divisions in American Jewry's religious community: Reform, Conservative, and Orthodox. Within Orthodoxy significant subdivisions exist, mostly of a more traditional nature, like *Agudath Yisroel* or the *Lubavitcher chassidim*, who maintain their independence from structures of mainline Orthodox Judaism. They make their policy decisions independently.

Within the three main denominations decisions on social policy matters are made separately. It is not unusual for the congregational and rabbinic bodies to take separate and sometimes varying positions, though consultation is frequent and assumed. The congregational bodies formulate policy usually through resolutions which are presented and voted on at regularly scheduled assemblies of their delegated representatives. In the rabbinic world a similar process takes place at rabbinic conventions. These adopted resolutions become the mandates under which representatives or spokespersons of the different religious agencies operate. For example, to my knowledge Orthodox Judaism never either supported or opposed César Chávez's boycott of grapes and lettuce, because neither of Orthodoxy's arms took official positions on the subject. Reform Judaism, on the other hand, did endorse Chávez's boycott but only after resolutions of support were introduced and passed at the national conventions of both the rabbinic and congregational bodies.

The Synagogue Council of America is an umbrella of the three mainstream religious communities. It is composed, however, of six agencies: the rabbinic and congregational arms of each of the three groups. The SCA makes its policy decision on social issues through unanimity arrived at among the six groups meeting in plenary session. Each has the right to veto any proposed policy. The veto has been used infrequently. Interestingly, where one of the agencies has no policy on a specific issue it might permit the SCA to take a position.

Let us apply this process to a specific issue: abortion. How does the Jewish religious community feel about "freedom of choice?" By and large the Reform and Conservative movements support legislation protecting or insuring a woman's right to choose a therapeutic abortion. Both movements have resolutions to this affect. Orthodox

Judaism would be less inclined to give public support to such legislation. The SCA takes no formal stand on the matter.

Similarly, in the area of church-state separation and federal aid for parochial schools, Reform and Conservative Judaism take stands more strongly supporting the status quo of separation, opposing attempts to further widen the parameters for more federal aid to parochial schools. The Orthodox community would be less endorsing of this posture.

Would it be fair to say that American religious Jewry is split on such subjects? Yes and no! If resolutions were the determinative measure, the answer might be given in the affirmative. But if numbers of Jews were the measure, the conclusions might be—and I suggest, are—seen differently. Using this latter criterion of numbers, I believe that the majority within the American Jewish community more broadly tolerates freedom of choice and is less inclined further to erode the wall of separation between church and state. How does one come to this conclusion? The answer lies in looking beyond just the posture of the Jewish *religious* community and to the Jewish community as a whole, as it is seen through the prism of nonreligious organized Jewry.

The Larger Jewish Community

The National Jewish Community Relations Advisory Council is an umbrella body consisting of all national Jewish organizations and 106 local Jewish Community Relations Councils drawn from almost every community in the country containing an organized Jewish community. The national organizations which belong to the NJCRAC are: B'nai B'rith–ADL, the American Jewish

Committee, the American Jewish Congress, Hadassah, Women's American ORT, the Jewish War Veterans, the Jewish Labor Committee, the National Council of Jewish Women, the Union of Orthodox Jewish Congregations, the United Synagogue of America, the Union of American Hebrew Congregations. The rabbinic bodies participate in the NJCRAC process through an instrumentality known as the Joint Advisory Committee. The NJCRAC is possibly the most broadly representative consortium in American Jewish life. Each local Community Relations Council is itself a body representative of the Jewish organizations in its own community. Each national organization and/or Community Council that belongs to the NJCRAC does so voluntarily.

The NJCRAC is primarily a process. It is advisory in nature, with strong emphasis on community consultation, coordination, and joint policy formation. The Plenary is the ultimate policy formulation body of the NJCRAC. It meets annually as a delegated body with representatives from each of the member national agencies and from each local Community Relations Council. Between annual meetings an elected Executive Committee meets three times a year. The Executive is formed with balanced representation from national and local member agencies. In addition the NJCRAC researches issues and recommends policies through five standing commissions. They report either to the Executive or to the Plenary. The scope of the NJCRAC's concerns is reflected in the titles and mandates of those five commissions, they are the commissions on:

1. Church State and Interreligious Affairs.
2. Equal Opportunity. This commission deals primarily with social justice issues.
3. Individual Freedom and Jewish Security. Civil rights and liberties as well as anti-Semitism are the chief interests of this commission.

4. Israel.

5. International Jewish Community Affairs. Concern with the situation of Jews in other lands, such as Syria, the Soviet Union, Latin America, the Falashas, etc., are the interests of this commission.

The NJCRAC process is a meticulous one. Its study documents reflect the best thinking of some of American Jewry's leading experts, and its annual Joint Program Plan is a superb distillation of the thinking and expertise of the American Jewish community. It merits careful study by anyone wanting to know what the American Jewish community is thinking and what it recommends on issues that range from anti-Semitism and Skokie, to parochial aid and support for the Humphrey-Hawkins bill.

The Council of Jewish Federations (CJF)

The NJCRAC was created in 1944 as a result of a call for the establishment of such a coordinating process issued by the Council of Jewish Federations. The CJF, established in 1932, is the national service body of the local Jewish federations. As early as the 1890s two communities, Boston and Cincinnati, saw the need to coordinate the work of then separate fund-raising organizations in their communities. The result was the generation of the first Jewish federations. Parenthetically, these became the prototype of what is now known in the general world as The United Way. The federation idea grew rapidly. There are approximately 220 Jewish federations in the U.S. and Canada. About 200 are affiliated with the CJF.

Federations today see themselves as organizations responsible for the entire Jewish population in a given geographic area. They have grown in influence, partially due to the mergers in various communities of local federations and Jewish Welfare Funds, which primarily raised philanthropic monies for overseas needs. Federations coordinate Jewish fund raising and disbursement in a local community and promote maintenance of Jewish life both here and abroad. Obviously the dispersal of such funds (and in larger Jewish communities the amounts are substantial, in some instances exceeding ten to fifteen million dollars per annum) requires careful budgeting and social planning. The national offices of the Council of Jewish Federations coordinates and guides such planning, besides initiating and supervising social welfare projects locally and nationally. When, for example, a disastrous flood engulfed Wilkes Barre, Pennsylvania, several years ago, devasting a large section of the community—in which were found a substantial number of Jewish families, as well as the Jewish Community Center and some of the community's religious institutions—the CJF sent in teams of experts who worked with local Jewish leadership and agencies of local and state governments to help restore the life of the community.

The need to maintain good working relationships with the agencies of a Jewish community is obvious. That effort is made constantly. Likewise, close contacts and liaison are kept between local federations and the local Community Relations Council, which is also financed in part by the CJF. The determination of social policies for a local community is usually delegated to a Community Relations Council, which in turn brings into an active, participatory role as many of the structures of the Jewish community, both lay and religious, as can be persuaded to participate. Few indeed are the local Jewish community structures that remain outside this coordinating process. Not only do they wish to influence policy formation on the local and then the national level, they also are the recipients of financial allocations made by the local federations' allocations committees. It is interesting to note that in most communities, local synagogues do not receive federation assistance. However, it is not unusual for Orthodox religious day schools to receive Jewish community funds, allocations from a local federation.

The General Assembly of the CJF meets annually to determine policy for the parent organization. Federations are becoming increasingly powerful in American Jewish life. In some communities there is a growing friction between the federation and synagogues which do not feel sufficiently involved or heeded in the policy-making process of the local community. The areas in which federations and Welfare Funds have particular policy expertise are those of social welfare and health. In conjunction with other agencies of the Jewish community, it is not unlikely that CJF will make policy decisions in such matters as financing for homes for the aged, funds for immigrants to this country, or in specific health matters, such as legislation affecting the Hill-Burton Act, etc.

The Jewish Welfare Board

In addition to social service, social action advocacy, health and welfare institutions, the Jewish community has created structures for the cultural and recreational needs of its adults and youth. Jewish Centers are to be found in most sizeable Jewish communities and many own or operate summer camps for Jewish youth. The planning for and the coordination of the activities of these agencies falls largely under the aegis of the Jewish Welfare Board. It also coordinates the work of the Jewish chaplaincy, both civil and military. The JWB is not primarily a policy-making instrument of the Jewish community, though it does make decisions in areas of its own expertise.

Jewish Education

The American Jewish community has an elaborate structure for the Jewish education of its young. Most youth are educated through the synagogues, all of whose national bodies maintain rather elaborate departments or divisions of education. These produce texts and curricula for the schools of their denomination. In addition, however, there exists an overall national coordinating educational agency, the American Association of Jewish Education. It serves as a coordinating and resource center for any and all wishing its help. In addition, it services local bureaus of Jewish education and seeks to develop schools in major centers of Jewish population for the training of teachers. As a coordinating and service agency, the association does not involve itself in special policy decision making.

Even such a cursory overview of the structure of the American Jewish community reveals its complexity as well as the breadth of its concerns and outreach. It has been said repeatedly that the Jewish community is perhaps the most overorganized structure in the world. That may be. The Jewish community has been an organized one for nearly four millenia. It is the way we have survived in a world which often excluded, sometimes ignored, and occasionally threatened, our existence. Survivalistic self-interest dictated much of our structuring, and that too has shaped the formation of many of our policies. The conclusions to which we have come, the decisions to which we come in the future, may not always be correct, but they will not suffer from lack of the most thoughtful and detailed kind of consideration.

Social Policy-Making Structures of the United States Catholic Conference

FRANCIS J. LALLY

WITHIN THE LARGE PICTURE to be considered in this discussion—Religious Traditions and Social Policy—my paper is designed to limit itself to the process now functioning at the USCC/NCCB by which statements on social policy come into being. It is necessary to know in broad outline the way the Conference organization is established in order to understand how the process works within that structure. Let me outline this in very general terms.

The Conference is, broadly speaking, the body of bishops who are functioning in the Church structures, largely dioceses, in the United States. The officers of the Conference are elected by the body of bishops for terms of three years. This body meets twice a year for a period of two or three days—once in Washington and once in Chicago.

For operational reasons an Administrative Board is elected from the membership, and this body meets four times annually. An Executive Committee is also formed to act between meetings, and this is composed mainly of Conference officers.

During the year, the Conference is directed by a General Secretary and staff, who work in Washington. The Conference is itself divided into the National Conference of Catholic Bishops (NCCB) and the United States Cath-

15

olic Conference (USCC). The NCCB concerns itself largely with ecclesiastical matters: seminary training, priestly ministry, ecumenical affairs, liturgy, and so forth. The USCC deals with so-called "civil" questions, and under this heading would come matters of social policy. These divisions do not represent any real exclusivity, since most questions reach into several Conference departments.

Against this broad background let us turn now to the question of statements emanating from the Conference. The general membership issues four kinds of statements: pastorals, formal statements, special messages, and resolutions. These are merely convenient titles for the variety of public pronouncements which may be required on one occasion or another. Besides these, the Conference also speaks through its Executive Committee, Administrative Board, President, General Secretary, and occasionally through Conference committees. It is understandable that the public which receives these statements rarely makes much of a distinction regarding their source; the divisions are organizationally important but practically of little consequence. It is hardly necessary to say that this array of statement sources is a matter of recurring confusion; it is even now under study and review by a Conference committee.

We come now to the process by which a statement evolves. This subject is dealt with in an Appendix to the Conference Bylaws:

What process is to be employed in preparing the document?

A statement can be drafted in many different ways. It can be written by one author. It can be divided into sections and each section can be written by a different person. It can be written from the start by a bishop or bishops. It can be drafted by a consultant or consultants and submitted for review to a committee of bishops. It can be prepared through a process of extremely wide consultation at the national and local levels; consultation can be restricted to a small number of specialists in the field being treated; or there can be no consultation at all. Circumstances will dictate the process—including the time available, the purpose or purposes of the documents, the preexistence (or non-existence) of widespread consensus in the Catholic community regarding the subject matter, etc. Insofar as possible, a process should be devised and implemented which is suited to the exigencies of this particular document. Also, in the future it may prove increasingly desirable to provide interested individuals and organizations outside the bishops' conference with drafts of major documents and invite them to submit their criticisms and suggestions for revision—without, of course, guaranteeing that their views will prevail. Among other things, such a procedure is likely to increase the acceptance of bishops' statements among concerned parties.[1]

Now let me describe the normal chronology of a statement as I see it developing within the Conference.

First there is the *subject* for comment. How is the topic arrived at?

The subject for discussion normally arises from one of four sources:

(1) proposed by the body of bishops at a semiannual meeting

(2) proposed by department committees (each department has an advisory committee which, for NCCB departments, is made up only of bishops; for USCC, it is made up of bishops and laity).

(3) proposed by the Advisory Council (a national committee of lay and clergy members, meeting twice yearly, which advises the Administrative Board on programming and other matters).

(4) proposed by staff (normally this would pass through the departmental committee, but not necessarily).

(From whichever of these sources a topic takes its origin,

it must proceed, if time allows, to the Administrative Board for its approval and direction. After appropriate discussion, the topic, if approved, is directed for action to the appropriate department or departments within the Conference.

Now let us discuss the matter of *procedure*: How is the subject moved forward? (We are still discussing the *process* mechanism to produce a statement.)

The department chairman, always a bishop, appoints a subcommittee to inaugurate action on the proposed statement. He first turns to members of his own committee, one of whom normally becomes chairman of the subcommittee. Working with staff, the subcommittee chairman selects other Conference staff familiar with the subject, available experts in the field (often from the academic world), and theological advisors identified with this topic.

The resulting subcommittee meets to determine the design of the statement. Is the approach a wide-ranging survey or does it have specific aims? What aspect of the subject is relevant for episcopal comment? To what audience is it directed?

With these questions answered (or at least discussed), how will the statement proceed?

After subcommittee discussion, a draft or outline is prepared for comment. This may be done by a staff member or someone appointed by the committee. The draft is then circulated to subcommittee members for review. A wider circle of interested parties is now involved, the size depending on the nature of the statement. This review may include opposite numbers in the ecumenical establishment or independent non-Catholic resources.

At this point the statement receives committee approval as a "working text." The text is next reviewed by the full departmental committee, and comments are solicited. It is also circulated among the concerned departments within the Conference. After this, it must receive approval by the departmental committee before being sent to the Administrative Board.

The Administrative Board receives the statement, determines at what level it should be issued, and directs its publication. It may be modified, returned to the committee for revision, or it may be rejected, or it may be presented to the body of bishops for action.

Thus ends the normal process by which a statement of the Conference on social policy evolves. Now let us turn to the *methodology* within the subcommittee. How is the topic discussed there, and what resources or guidelines are used?

The working committee first discusses the topic itself as a subject for public comment by the Conference. It is timely and a matter of wide public concern? Some of this will already have been indicated when the topic is first proposed for action. Now it will be studied in greater depth. Is it suitable for an episcopal statement? Does the Church, as Church, have something important to say on this matter? Is guidance needed at this time? Will the statement assist public education and contribute to dialogue?

Next, the specific religious concern must be identified. Do the ethical or moral implications come through clearly? Where does it fit into the broader theological picture? Is the community in need of guidance on this issue? What resources are here and now available to assist in giving it a religious perspective?

At this point, the subcommittee seeks to discover what has already been said on the subject. Does Scripture or the Church Councils or traditional Church teachings speak to the topic? What of encyclicals, synods, and Church directives? Are there earlier statements by bishops, or does it form a part of Catholic social teaching? Have other episcopal conferences spoken on the issue? What about other religious groups, specialists in the field, or academics?

With these questions considered, it is appropriate to apply Catholic social teaching (insofar as it exists in the area considered) to the present concern. An analysis of the social context is usually required, as well as a definition of the issues under discussion in this context. From this, the practical relevance of Church teaching is outlined and expounded, and implications for the audience are described. The subject must also be viewed in its institutional significance for the Church and for society. Does it call for individual and social action? Where does it fit in the larger human and religious picture?

In this connection, the committee seeks out what elements of controversy may exist and how they should be treated. How will it be understood within the Church, among other religious bodies, in the community generally? What elements of reconciliation can be emphasized?

Finally, the committee considers publication and distribution. Will it reach those for whom it is intended? How? How will it be used in the mass media, the religious media? Will it have application locally? Should study outlines be supplied for schools or for adults?

Needless to say, not every statement follows the full outline described here. Some topics must be prepared more quickly; some have already been pretty much outlined in earlier positions; some are expressed by the President or General Secretary rather than the full Conference. Moreover, there is nothing that precludes a change in the present manner of operation. The process continues to be revised and could be altered by the Conference whenever more effective operations are offered.

NOTE

1. National Conference of Catholic Bishops/United States Catholic Conference, "Statutes and Bylaws" (July, 1976), p. 50.

II. Religion and Family Policy

Introduction

IN THIS FIRST OF the "representative issues" which form
the heart of the discussion, the authors are asked: How
does your community draw on its religious tradition in
developing a response to the question of whether the
American government should adopt a national family
policy?

The different manner in which the two authors respond
to this question establishes a pattern that will be evinced
consistently in the remainder of the papers. It is not that
the ultimate values evoked differ greatly. Both go back to
a common Hebrew scriptural heritage. Nor is it that the
social policy implications are in conflict. The papers and
the discussion reveal remarkably similar senses of the role
of the family and its needs and crises today. Rather, the
ethical processes involved in interpreting the question itself and in moving from biblical values to contemporary
applications are reflective of the styles of moral and religious thinking that have been developed by our two an-
cient communities throughout (and in reaction to) their
histories.

Bishop Stafford centers on the methodological considerations. Taking a recent instance of family policy issued

by the National Conference of Catholic Bishops, the "Plan of Pastoral Action for Family Ministry," Bishop Stafford seeks to surface the religious values underlying the concrete actions that plan recommends. In this process, Bishop Stafford, who chaired the committee which prepared the document, deals with a set of social principles drawn from papal and conciliar sources, especially "natural law." His is thus an exercise in ecclesial hermeneutics, in how the Church's understanding evolves and adapts its stance to changing empirical insights. Scripture is not directly applied to the modern situation, but its values are applied as "mediated" through these traditional principles.

Rabbi Siegel begins immediately to grapple with the question itself. He first describes the general view of the family in the Hebrew Bible and in the Talmud. This understanding he applies directly in a critique of four areas of current government policy, which in some degree seem "to be contrary to the basic outlook of traditional [Jewish] religion": population control, education, the role of women, and biological research. In each of these areas, Rabbi Siegel adduces relevant portions of traditional Jewish attitudes and practice (*halachah*).

Traditionally, both communities have distinguished between the society and the state. The common good, the quest for justice, is a higher (or broader) good than public order, which is the function of the state. The family, not the state, is the primary educator of public morality. The Catholic experience, deeply influenced until recent times by the European context of its official statements, has been characterized by a sense of mistrust of governmental action, especially in the cultural or value sphere. Similarly, a major thrust of Jewish life in America has been to resist governmental involvement in the life of the family and in the realm of personal values.

In the minds of many religious analysts of social policy

today, this sense of caution is mixed with a feeling that there is a need for the government to undertake programs that will affirm the value of the family and support family life. Given the deep commitment of both religious communities to family life, a commitment intensified by similar experiences of immigrant life in this country, there is a sense that the area of the family provides an opportunity for close collaboration and joint action between Jewish and Catholic agencies. Such cooperation, if effective, may aid in improving not only the quality of life of these two communties, but all American families.

Religion and Family Policy:
A Catholic Perspective

J. FRANCIS STAFFORD

THE QUESTION OF HOW the Roman Catholic community
moves to the establishment of a social policy based on
its belief in the sanctity of the family is more than a
theoretical issue. In June 1975, the Committee on Education of the United States Catholic Conference, acting on
the proposal of the Administrative Board of that Conference, established an ad hoc commission "to study and
make recommendations to the national Church on a comprehensive strategy of intervention on the part of the
Church at all levels to support and strengthen the vocation of marriage and family life."[1] Three years later, in
May 1978, the United States Catholic Bishops voted to
accept the recommendations of this commission. They
issued the "Plan of Pastoral Action for Family Ministry"
and placed it under the charge of the newly established
Commission of Marriage and Family Life, of which I
am chairperson.

The burden of this paper will be to discuss the method
by which this Plan for Family Ministry (as I shall refer to
it here) was developed. This plan is concerned especially
with ministry to families within the Roman Catholic community; it also addresses the importance of the Church's
social mission to families and points to practical areas of

concern. The plan does not address in depth the questions: "Should the United States government establish a national family policy?" or "What should be the nature of such a policy?" or "How shall the Roman Catholic community respond to such a policy?" Rather, this document introduces and encourages an important way of addressing and sounding out questions of social policy and social mission with regard to family issues. It does provide a concrete example of the way the Roman Catholic community goes about translating its beliefs into social policy. The resources and processes operative in the establishment of this plan would likewise come into play in a Roman Catholic response to any governmental policy.[2]

What is more, the committee that developed this plan did not work with an explicitly chosen and delineated methodology. Had they done so, this paper would of course have been much easier to prepare. On the other hand, the unconscious nature of the methodology underlying this plan provides a valuable insight into the Roman Catholic mind as it moves from belief to policy. For once the operative presuppositions and procedures of the plan are teased out, we gain an understanding of the normal—one might say natural—paths we are accustomed to follow in thinking about and acting on issues such as the family.

The Plan for Family Ministry fundamentally focusses on a process, engaging the Church at all levels to address effectively the broad spectrum of family issues and needs. Its goal is to help the family at a time when it is beset by many difficulties; but it does so by calling upon the strengths that the family itself shows, and it utilizes those through a ministry and service of like-to-like, that is, of family-to-family. Toward that end it emphasizes: (1) education of people to the meaning of the family within the Roman Catholic community; (2) analysis and interpretation of the American culture as to its strengths and weaknesses for supporting the family; and (3) the ministry to families by families that flows from a sense of Christian mission. To achieve that end, educational procedures have been developed and support structures are being planned. 1980 has been designated Family Year, during which family values and ministry will be celebrated. We are in the process of preparation for that event. It is hoped that this "will usher in a decade of research into Christian marriage and family life and a time for the development of outstanding programs in family ministry."[3]

To understand the methodology which lies behind the development of the Plan for Family Ministry we must first of all consider some broader issues about the nature of the Roman Catholic community that are relevant to the matter at hand. The Roman Catholic community has never had a sectarian type of self-identity that would allow it to be either indifferent or hostile to the world within which it lives. It understands itself to be a part of the world, affected by it yet also seeking to affect that world, to work in it and with it to realize the fulness of God's dominion on earth. This was probably best expressed by one of the documents of the Second Vatican Council: "The joys and the hopes, the griefs and the anxieties of the men of this age, especially those who are poor or in any way afflicted, these too are the joys and hopes, the griefs and anxieties of the followers of Christ."[4]

The full significance of this dialogical interchange with a secular society is only gradually impacting the Roman Catholic community in the United States. In the words of Father John L. Thomas, S.J., a Roman Catholic sociologist,

> . . . a minority can retain its religious minority identity either by isolating itself from the alien influences of the dominant culture, as some groups such as the Mennonites are striving to do, or by selective integration.

American Catholics have always opted for the latter solution, but until the last few decades the major portion of them remained relatively isolated, owing to their ethnic and regional urban concentration, immigrant and culturally alien origins, and related socio-economic status. This incidental form of isolation is rapidly ceasing to exist, with the result that Catholics are beginning to experience the full impact of their increasingly secularized social environment.[5]

It is this change in the status of the American Roman Catholic that has provided both the problem and an important dimension of the solution delineated in the Plan for Family Ministry. Selective integration requires the maintenance of one's own distinctive values while at the same time respecting and taking seriously the values of secular society. This has serious implications for the type of methodology the Roman Catholic community uses to develop its social policy, as will be shown later in this paper.

A second factor operative within the Roman Catholic community that is apropos to this discussion is the nature of that community itself. Prior to the Second Vatican Council, it was customary both popularly and theologically to identify the Church primarily with its hierarchical structures—the pope, the bishops, the priests—and only secondarily with the laity. The Vatican Council, recovering an understanding which was a part of the Church earlier in its history, emphasized that membership in the Church comes not from ordination to priesthood but from baptism. Consequently, the Church is first and foremost the totality of its membership.[6] The members of the hierarchy are ordained into an order of service as ministers who "work for the good of the whole body" by looking to its "nurturing and constant growth."[7]

This recovered appreciation of the place of the laity in the Church, of their centrality in the mission of the Church to join with God in the establishment of his dominion in the world, laid the foundation for a renewed concern for the family, and even more for a deeper insight into the important role of the family in the realization of the Church's mission.

A third factor, one related to this renewed understanding of the Church, is an appreciation of the importance of dealing with issues in a decentralized way at the most subordinate level possible. In 1971, Pope Paul VI, speaking about the application of Roman Catholic social teaching to specific issues, made the following statements:

> In the face of . . . widely varying situations it is difficult for us to utter a unified message and to put forward a solution which has universal validity. Such is not our ambition, nor is it our mission. It is up to the Christian communities to analyze with objectivity the situation which is proper to their own country, to shed on it the light of the Gospel's unalterable words and to draw principles of reflection, norms of judgment and directives for action from the social teaching of the Church. This social teaching has been worked out in the course of history and notably, in this industrial era, since the historic date of the message of Pope Leo XIII on "the condition of the workers," and it is an honour and joy for us to celebrate today the anniversary of that message. It is up to these Christian communities, with the help of the Holy Spirit, in communion with the bishops who hold responsibility and in dialogue with other Christian brethren and all men of good will, to discern the options and commitments which are called for in order to bring about the social, political and economic changes seen in many cases to be urgently needed.[8]

The Plan for Family Ministry is the response of the Roman Catholic community in the United States to that challenge. The message of the Scriptures and principles drawn from the tradition of the Church have been applied critically to the concrete historical situation of our society. Bishops, priests, and laity have joined together in an ongoing dialogue "to decipher authentic signs of God's presence and purpose in the happenings, needs, and desires"[9] experienced by people within this society. The results of this dialogue, joined with a realistic assessment of the resources of the community and the possibilities of the times, led to the formation of the Plan for Family Ministry.

Over and above this, the decentralized approach to social issues is further evidenced in the dynamics of the plan itself. It calls for a ministry to families carried out by families themselves, i.e., for a ministry performed at the most subordinate level possible.

We must now look more closely at the sources which the Roman Catholic community draws upon in establishing its social policy. In his statement cited earlier, Pope Paul VI says that this policy is grounded in "light of the Gospel's unalterable words" and the "principles of reflection, norms of judgment and directives for action from the social teaching of the Church."[10] In point of fact, the Plan for Family Ministry does not draw immediately and directly on scriptural material. It contains the following statement: "At the outset we affirm that the faithful proclamation of the Gospel in word and sacrament is fundamental to all such planning in the church."[11] But at no time is there any direct reference to the Scriptures either in the text itself or in the footnotes. This does not mean that the plan totally ignores the message of Scripture; rather there seems to be a practice of responding to and incorporating the message of Scripture as that has been mediated through the various papal, conciliar, and synodal statements—that is to say, as it has been mediated through the official documents of the Church. The concern of the community, at least as evidenced through the Plan for Family Ministry, is to remain faithful to the truths of our founding documents as they have been interpreted by the community itself.

The same appears to be the case for the other font of moral wisdom the Roman Catholic community has traditionally drawn upon: natural law. While the term "natural law" admits of no easy or single definition, it refers in general to that source of moral insight discovered by disciplined reflection on human experience and not directly dependent on the moral teaching of the Scriptures. It is grounded in our belief that we can discern something of God's purposes for humankind by looking at the deepest aspirations we experience in the course of the events of history. The plan never mentions natural law as such, but it definitely draws upon this type of moral wisdom as it has been taken up into our tradition and mediated through various official statements.[12]

Thus the primary source the plan draws upon for its principles is the official statements issued by the leadership of the Roman Catholic community, especially the documents of the Second Vatican Council as well as various declarations by the pope or by groups of bishops.

But the methodology used in developing the Plan for Family Ministry is not entirely deductive in nature; empirical input is an essential component. This is seen by following the history of the development of the plan. The concern expressed by the Roman Catholic community about the problems besetting the family that eventuated in the establishment of the ad hoc commission to work out a comprehensive plan for family ministry did not originate in the principles stated by a conciliar or a papal document. It grew out of the concrete experience of Roman Catholic living in the United States: experience of a loss of "relative family stability, . . . of divorce, abortion, teenage pregnancy and the general breakdown of family values."[13]

In the early stages of the development of the plan, twelve regional meetings were held at which family life directors from dioceses across the country "surfaced issues and priorities regarding family and marriage and evaluated present educational programs."[14] More input came from the "Call to Action" conference sponsored by the United States bishops and held in Detroit in the fall of 1976. This conference, called at the time of our national bicentennial, was the culmination of a nationwide dialogue within the Roman Catholic community which had as its purpose to unite people "in the widest possible sharing of assessments of how the American Catholic community can contribute to the quest of all people for liberty and justice."[15] That conference also targeted the family as an area of primary concern for the Roman Catholic community.

A final source of empirical input in developing the Plan for Family Ministry was a scientific sociological study on the status of the family in the United States. This research, carried out by Dr. William McCready[16] of the National Opinion Research Center, played an important role in the establishment of the plan in its final state by calling attention to the strengths of the family and the importance of on-going research.

Still, it seems evident from the methodology used by the commission in working out the plan that the scientific information provided by sociology through its statistical procedures does not have the final word. It was taken up within the belief and value systems of the Roman Catholic community and there interpreted and evaluated; only then did it have significance for the establishment of social policy. This also explains the importance given to the testimony of the diocesan family life directors and of the people who participated in the bicentennial Call to Action.

Of importance to the community in working out its social policy is the meaning of the times as seen through the eyes of faith, of the events occuring within a particular society as interpreted by a community of people whose members have been formed by and imbued with its traditions.

Thus, the Plan for Family Ministry is much more than a secular social policy. It is essentially theological, both in its grounding and in its framing, and as such it is more in the nature of a program for pastoral practice, representing the community's active concern for the spiritual well-being of its members and, indeed, of all people.

To sum up thus far, the national policies affecting the family established by the Roman Catholic community have been worked out within a community that is conscious of its ties to and responsibilities for the world in which it lives; that has been awakened to a new understanding of the nature of membership; that is newly aware of the responsibility of each segment within it to respond to the specific needs of its own society and generation. The resources it depended upon in developing this policy are, on the one hand, the wisdom of the Scriptures and of natural law as mediated through the recent official documents of the Church and, on the other, empirical insight into the meanings and difficulties of the present time as provided by both scientific and nonscientific sources and interpreted in light of the community's faith commitments.

We must now consider the actual dynamics by which the principles taken from the Church's official documents were interrelated to the experiential data drawn from the various empirical sources.

The relationship that exists between these two sources is one of dynamic and complementary interdependence and dialectical interchange. Each source plays an essential role in arriving at the end product: the social policy. They are correlated in such a way that each at once challenges and complements the other, and from their correlation, a final stance is evolved.

More concretely, in the Plan for Family Ministry, the principles enunciated in the official documents of the Church initially acted as a negative principle in the discussions leading to the establishment of the policy. They circumscribed the area within which the discussion was to take place, not indicating positively the subject matter to be investigated or the conclusions to be reached, but disclosing those areas where the Roman Catholic community has taken definitive positions representing its self-understanding at this point in its history.

Evidence of this is to be found in the response made by the American bishops to the Call to Action conference in Detroit. At that conference, many issues were surfaced as demanding the attention of the Roman Catholic community. Among these was a recommendation about change in the Church's stance concerning the ordination of women.[17] The bishops responded that, in light of the Church's official stance on this matter, they could not consider the possibility of altering the Church's position.[18] The official position of the Roman Catholic community provided a limiting horizon within which the discussion of issues was to take place.

This is not to say that the limiting horizon established by the official teaching of the community is immobile. The Second Vatican Council has made the Roman Catholic community aware of the historically conditioned nature of its structures, formulations, and practices.[19] But changes are always evolutionary in nature, containing within them substantive continuities with the past, with the core of beliefs that are the foundation of the community. Thus, for example, at one point in our history, it was held to be immoral to seek to make a profit on the loaning of money. Such was a serious sin against jus-tice; and this position had strong, authoritative backing. But changes in society, particularly in its economic struc-tures, initiated a reassessment, and the community came to see that it could remain constant in its commitment to justice only by altering its discipline.[20] At the present time there is a change occuring in the Roman Catholic community's position on private property. In 1891 Pope Leo XIII in his famous encyclical *On the Condition of Workers* declared that private property is a natural right possessed by each person which the State can not sup-press.[21] But beginning with Pope John XXIII, a change in thought begins to appear, brought about by a growing awareness of the multiplication and increasing complexity of social relations within a highly industrialized and tech-nological society. And, in the words of one commentator, "Paul VI erodes any primacy of ownership by his develop-ment goal of *being* more human rather than *having* more goods. Also, he moves from economics toward the pri-macy of *political power* for transforming societal struc-tures."[22] Throughout all this, the concern of the Roman Catholic community remains constant: to ensure to all people sufficient living conditions so that they can achieve their own perfection.

More to the point of this discussion on the family, changes in society are having a definite impact within the Roman Catholic community in the definition of the purpose of marriage. From the time of St. Augustine up to the present century, discussion centered on the *bona* or the goods served by marriage. This grew out a a mind-set which was uneasy with human sexuality and found in the goals of marriage a means of legitimating it. It is only in this century that the Roman Catholic community ana-lyzed more thoroughly the *fines* or ends of marriage. And, whereas the discussion of the ends of marriage originally referred to a hierarchy with the procreative dimensions primary and the unitive secondary, the Second Vatican Council maintained the importance of both ends but refused to rank one over the other.[23]

Thus, the official teaching of the Church does develop; but it does so only slowly—after much dialogue and in response to distinctive historical-social shifts. Until such time as this occurs, it provides a limiting horizon circumscribing the boundaries within which social policy is to be established.

Within the parameters thus mapped out, there is a second instance of the use of the principle of correlation. On a more positive note, the official teaching of the Church provides "principles of reflection, norms of judgment and directives for action."[24] But these are multiple and varied; at issue here is the procedure by which certain of these are chosen and others are not. Selection is made in light of the demands of the concrete situation as established through empirical input. These demands determine the relevance of certain principles.

This is evident at various points in the Plan for Family Ministry. First of all, as mentioned earlier, the very fact that the family was selected as a primary concern upon which the Roman Catholic community should focus its time, energy, and resources grew out of the experience of the community—an experience which pointed to the difficulties presently facing the family. The very fact that the plan as finally established emphasizes the ministerial service of the family, the ability of the family to make positive contributions to the mission of the Church in the American context, the ability of the family to engage in like-to-like ministry grew out of the empirical evidence. This showed that, while the family is seriously beset by many and deep difficulties within the American context, it also evidences a strength within our society in that it shows no signs of disappearing and in fact has certain internal strengths which can be drawn upon. This served to highlight the positive principles and directives regarding the family to be found in the official teaching of the Church. As a result, great emphasis is placed on the statement in one of the documents of Vatican II that "the family is . . . the domestic Church":[25] This would make little or no sense if the only experience the Roman Catholic community had of the family within our society was negative.

At the same time, the relationship between the empirical evidence and the official teaching of the Church is not simply a one-way street; the principle of correlation is still very much in evidence. As was mentioned earlier, the Roman Catholic community does not establish social policy in response to bare, uninterpreted facts. Empirical evidence must be taken up into a system of interpretation and evaluation. Thus, in establishing the general thrust of the Plan for Family Ministry, the fact that the strengths rather than the weaknesses and difficulties of the family ultimately were the center of focus was itself the result of certain ways of understanding the family which are intrinsic to the Roman Catholic community and very much in evidence in its official teaching. The Church holds marriage to be a sacrament, and the family itself to be the "domestic church"—realities which, in the deepest sense of that term involve God's saving action in history. In living out their marriage in the fullest manner possible, the spouses incarnate the saving presence of God in his Church and give flesh to his continuing concern to realize the dominion of God in the world. As such, the Roman Catholic community necessarily holds marriage to be central to the religious process. Added to this is the emphasis given by the Second Vatican Council to the centrality of the laity in the Church and to the importance of the local Church. All of this provided a "hermeneutical circle," if you will, within which the value and meaning of the strength of the family, established experientially, could be understood and accepted.

This I believe to be the heart of the process by which the Roman Catholic community moves from its beliefs to social policy. It works within a horizon established by the community that discloses its fundamental commitments at a given point in history. While these are by no means considered to be totally unchanging and beyond question, they evolve only gradually after much dialogue and in response to significantly different historical and social milieux. Within this horizon, the principles and directives offered by the official teaching and the experimental situation of a given segment of the Roman Catholic community are correlated with one another. Each challenges and illuminates the other; and out of this a social policy is set which is tested by its ability to respond to the concrete situation in which the community finds itself.

At the end of the Plan for Family Ministry explicit recognition is given to the official documents from which were drawn the principles used to establish the parameters of the discussion and to interpret and evaluate data.[26] In so doing, we acknowledge and reaffirm the continuity and faithfulness of the American Church with the international Roman Catholic community.

As should be evident from the discussion of the methodology used in establishing the Plan for Family Ministry, there is no single and isolated point at which the religious element enters in; it is present from the beginning and is pervasive throughout the process. What distinguishes this approach to the establishment of a national social policy from that taken by a sociologist is that at no time do we ignore the ultimacy of faith in locating principles, working with empirical evidence, or establishing policy. The commitments we hold as a Roman Catholic community provide a means of interpretation and evaluation that is constantly operative. But this approach does not commit us to a deductive approach in working out our social policy. Empirical evidence plays an essential role in this process, a role that is at once constructive and critical. But never does it operate in isolation from or independently of the official teaching of the Church.

The importance of this methodology for translating our beliefs into social policy is that, while it allows us to remain faithful to our tradition, it also permits us to continue to respond to the world of which we are a part in the same spirit exhibited by the Second Vatican Council. As one document of that Council clearly and forthrightly states: "Hence in the light of Christ, the image of the unseen God, the firstborn of every creature, the Council wishes to speak to all men in order to illuminate the mystery of man and to cooperate in finding the solution to the outstanding problems of our times."[27]

The methodology underlying the Plan for Family Ministry provides the Roman Catholic community with a means of establishing both the theoretical and practical meaning of its beliefs in relation to the world and, in dialogue with those of differing faith commitments about the problems facing humankind, to offer that meaning as its substantive contribution toward seeking a solution. At that same time, it permits the Roman Catholic community to engage in true dialogue, entering the discussion both as one who has a contribution to make and as one who can listen and learn.

NOTES

1. Department of Education, United States Catholic Conference, *Final Report on the United States Catholic Conference Ad Hoc Commission on Marriage and Family Life* (Washington, D.C., 1977), p. 2.

2. In moving from a faith stance to the establishment of and/or the response to a national family policy set by the United States government, there is, of course, the added difficulty of having to remain loyal to one's own commitments, while at the same time responding to a pluralistic society. Without going into the matter at length, some further factors involved are: (1) the principle of natural law which disposes the Roman Catholic community to enter into dialogue about the family with an openness to learn from other sources, even nonreligious ones; (2) the principle of the common good, which leads the community to view the dialogue not as a clash of opinions but as a common search for that which best promotes the full humanity of the community and of its individual members (see Heinrich A. Rommen, *The State in Catholic Thought* [St. Louis, Mo.: B. Herder Book Co., 1950], pp. 282–305; Jean-Yves Calvez, S.J., and Jacques Perrin, S.J., *The Church and Social Justice: The Social Teaching of the Popes from Leo XIII to Pius XII (1878–1958)* [Chicago: Henry Regnery Company, 1961], pp. 114–118; Merle Longwood, "The Common Good: An Ethical Framework for Evaluating Environmental Issues," *Theological Studies* 34 [September 1973]: 476–480); and (3) an acceptance that there is a distinction between public policy and public morality (see John Courtney Murray, *We Hold These Truths: Catholic Reflections on the American Proposition* [Garden City, N.Y.: Image Books, 1964], pp. 155–174).

3. U.S. Catholic Bishops, "Plan of Pastoral Action for Family Ministry," *Origins* 8 (May 25, 1978): 4.

4. Pastoral Constitution on the Church in the Modern World, art. 1, *The Documents of Vatican II*, ed. W. Abbott, S.J. (New York: Guild Press, 1966), pp. 199–200.

5. Cited in *Final Report*, p. 4.

6. Dogmatic Constitution on the Church, art. 9, *The Documents of Vatican II*, pp. 24–26.

7. Ibid., art. 18, p. 37.

8. Pope Paul VI, *Octogesima Adveniens*, art. 4, *The Gospel of Peace and Justice*, ed. Joseph Gremillion (Maryknoll, N.Y.: Orbis Books, 1976), p. 487.

9. Pastoral Constitution on the Church in the Modern World, art. 11, p. 209.

10. Pope Paul VI, *Octogesima Adveniens*, art. 4, p. 487.

11. "Plan of Pastoral Action for Family Ministry," p. 1.

12. See, for example, the introduction and Part 2, Chapter 1 of Pastoral Constitution on the Church in the Modern World.

13. Bishop J. Francis Stafford, "Background on the Bishops' Family Plan," *Origins* 8 (May 25, 1978): 8.

14. *Final Report*, p. 2.

15. Cited in *A. D. 1977* (Hyattsville, Md.: Quixote Center, 1977), p. 1.

16. William C. McCready, "American Catholics and the Family," mimeographed (Washington, D.C., 1976).

17. "Justice in the Church," *Origins* 6 (Nov. 4, 1976): 20.

18. U.S. Catholic Bishops, "A Response to the Call to Action," *Origins* 6 (May 19, 1977): 761.

19. "Thanks to the experience of past ages, the progress of the sciences, and the treasures hidden in the various forms of human culture, the nature of man himself is more clearly revealed and new roads to truth are opened. These benefits profit the Church, too. For, from the beginning of her history, she has learned to express the message of Christ with the help of the ideas and terminology of various peoples, and has tried to clarify it with the wisdom of philosophers, too" (Pastoral Constitution on the Church in the Modern World, art. 44, p. 246). See also Pope Paul VI, *Mysterium Ecclesiae*, art. 5, cited in Raymond Brown, *Biblical Reflections on Crises Facing the Church* (New York: Paulist Press, 1975), pp. 116–118.

20. Daniel C. Maguire, "Moral Absoutes and the Magisterium," in *Absolutes in Moral Theology?*, ed. Charles E. Curran (Washington, D.C.: Corpus Books, 1968), pp. 67–68.

21. Pope Leo XIII, *On the Condition of Workers*, arts. 11–17.

22. Gremillion, *The Gospel of Peace and Justice*, p. 34.

23. See E. Schillebeeckx, *Marriage: Secular Reality and Saving Mystery*, trans. N. D. Smith, 2 vols. (London: Sheed and Ward, 1965); Peter Go, "Sexuality in the Proclamation of Pius XII," in *Concilium, Religion in the Seventies*, eds. Franz Bockle and Jacques-Marie Pohier, vol. 100 (New York: Seabury Press, 1976), pp. 4–21.

24. Pope Paul VI, *Octogesima Adveniens*, art. 4, p. 487.

25. Dogmatic Constitution on the Church, art. 11, in *The Documents of Vatican II*, p. 29. See also Yves Congar, *Lay People in the Church*, trans. Donald Attwater (Westminster, Md.: The Newman Press, 1967), pp. 202–203.

26. "Plan of Pastoral Action for Family Ministry," p. 7.

27. Pastoral Constitution on the Church in the Modern World, art. 10, p. 209.

Religion and Family Policy:
A Jewish Perspective

SEYMOUR SIEGEL

GEORGE BERNARD SHAW, WHEN a student, was obliged to submit an essay every week in English composition. He was annoyed at the assignment. One time he turned in an essay entitled: Snakes in Ireland. The text of the essay was: "There are none."

The answer to the question posed in this paper, "Should the government have a family policy?" is, of course, "Yes."

The reason for this answer is obvious. The family is in trouble, and the government is the main source of funds for social and cultural causes. The government may be the home of lost causes, or rather causes that lose money— but in many cases it is the *only* home that some causes have.

The family is, of course, the foundation stone of human society. This is a common conviction of the Jewish and Christian traditions:

> The human family constitutes the beginning and the essential element of society. . . . Peace in society must depend upon peace in the family, and the order and harmony of rulers and ruled must directly be actualized from the order and harmony arising out of creative guidance and commensurate response in the family.[1]

In the Jewish tradition, the whole of the people of Israel is called a family: "Only you have I known amongst the Families of the world" (Amos 3:2).

The view of the family in Jewish tradition is formed by the biblical view of sexuality and the view of the proper relationship between parents and children.

The familiar account in Genesis of the creation of the human species observes that after God had brought forth the first man, He said: "It is not right that man should be alone. I will make him an aid fit for him. . . . Then God cast a deep sleep upon the man and when he was asleep He took one of his ribs and closed up the flesh at the spot. And God fashioned into a woman the rib that He had removed from the man, and He brought her to the man. . . . Thus it is that man leaves his father and mother and clings to his wife, and they become one flesh."[2]

The account of the creation of woman as emerging from Adam's rib suggested to the talmudic sages that man and woman are incomplete without relating one to the other. The man-woman relationship is paradigmatic of all human existence, which is "being-in-fellow-humanity" (*mitmenschlichkeit*). Man can realize himself only by relating to a Thou, who, though differentiated, is still flesh of his flesh, bone of his bone. Sexuality in humans is not a purely biological function. Though Adam apparently could discharge his sexual energy through other species, he could not find real satisfaction until he could achieve the mutuality of relationship with a fellow human being. Only by finding Eve, his fellow existent, could he find his humanity. The family, which promotes mutuality, permanence, and responsibility, then, is the vehicle for the fulfillment of true human sexuality. Helmut Thielicke in *The Ethics of Sex* points out: "If sexuality were merely a matter of physiological function (and thus a glandular problem) or merely a vehicle of reproduction (though again a biological function), it would be difficult to see why the partners should not be just as interchangeable as the bearers of other biological or mechanical functions, such as draft animals, for example, or machines."[3] Promiscuity is not the outcome of freedom, in this view. It is, rather, a sign of depersonalization and dehumanization. True fulfillment of libido comes when there is a total personal relationship.

The sexual encounter must entail the goal of procreation in some sense. This means that sexuality should also involve responsibility for its outcome. Man is not to be like the male of other species who fertilizes the female and then leaves. He and his mate are to be fruitful and multiply and to nurture and feed the young—that is, to found a family.

Thus the foundation of the family is based on the assertion that its parameters of mutuality, permanence, covenant, and responsibility are the indispensable elements of a true fulfillment of man's sexual nature. This means that the Jewish outlook is pro-natalist and stresses the requirement of education of the young through the family.

The Talmud outlines the commandments which the father and mother owe to the young: "The father is obligated toward his son to circumcize him, to redeem him, to teach him Torah, to provide him with a wife and to teach him a trade. Some say to teach him also how to swim" (Kiddushin 29a).

The family's responsibilities toward the young are not exhausted by merely providing for the physical needs of the child. This is taken for granted. The parents are also obligated to introduce children into the basic foundations of their faith; to enable them to live a productive and full life, both socially and economically; to train them to meet life's emergencies (that is the meaning of to teach them how to swim), and above all to educate them in Torah—so that the children will properly live in accordance with the tradition of their fathers and be loyal to the covenant which has defined Jewish self-understanding.

This brief analysis points up the main values that emerge when considering the biblical-talmudic view of sexuality and the family. The values to be pursued are: the preservation of the family as the unit which makes human-ness possible; the facilitating of the birth and nurture of children; the maintenance and encouragement of the educational function of the family as the vehicle for entry into the community of faith; the enabling of the parents to educate their children in the earning of a livelihood, in the protection of interests, and above all in education for living.

Clearly, any government policy which would further these values should be encouraged. A policy which makes it difficult to sustain the family's ends and goals should be rejected.

We have spoken about the foundation of the family as the efficient and effective expression of human sexuality. The other pole of the biblical view of the family concerns the duties of children toward parents. In the Ten Commandments only the parents are the objects of a command to honor. Neither God nor political authority demands *kavod*. God demands that we extend *kavod* to our parents. *Kavod*, which is related to a root meaning heavy or weighty, implies that the children should see in their parents individuals of importance and dignity. They should be taught to respect, revere, and take seriously what their parents say and do.

There are interesting reflections in the literature as to the reasons why the biblical commands are so insistent that children honor their parents. Honoring of parents is an expression of gratitude for having been brought into

the world. It is related to the honor of God, since by
honoring those who brought a person into the world, one
acknowledges the Creator of all things. One commentator
on the Bible, Isaac Abarbanel, asserts that the commandment to honor parents implies that honoring of what parents teach and stand for; thus the fulfillment of the commandment sanctifies the concept of tradition, which the
parents presumably hand down. This recognition of the
importance of what previous generations have taught in-
sures the continuous peaceful process of communal and
political life.

It is not only the providing of material help to parents
that is commanded, but also *reverence*—that is, to relate
to the parents with consideration and recognition of the
respect due them. It is not only *what* is provided for parents, but *how* it is provided that is vital. Thus, the rabbis
tell a parable in which a person served his father very expensive food but nevertheless did not merit the world to
come. There was another man who had his father grind
the millstones and did merit the world to come. In the
first instance, when the father asked the son where he pur-
chased the expensive food, the son responded with anger,
"Chew, old man, and don't ask!" Such a son loses all his
reward. In the second instance, a son put his father to
work grinding millstones in order to avoid his being con-
scripted by the king—the son going in his father's place.
Such a son, of course, merits the reward prepared for him
in the world to come. The point of this parable is that
the attitude with which we provide for the needs of those
dependent upon us is as important as what it is that we
provide.

The respect, reverence, and love which should charac-
terize the relationships between children and parents are
summarized in the words of the talmudic sage Rabbi
Yoseph, who, when hearing the sound of his mother's

approaching footsteps would say: "I will stand up to honor the arrival of the *Schechina* [God's Presence]" (Tractate Kiddushin 30b).

The biblical-rabbinic view of the family, then, is based on the presence of mutual responsibilities of parents and children. The parents have the responsibility to educate their offspring for effective and reverent living within society. This is an outcome of their having brought their children into the world. The children, on their part, have the responsibility to honor and revere their parents and to fulfill their needs when that is necessary. When these responsibilities are fulfilled, the family becomes a creative and secure unit within the larger society, assuring the continuity and growth of the community.

From the point of view of Jewish tradition, government policies which impinge on the lives and structures of families should have as their outcome the strengthening of the values which are the basis of the normative relationships between parents and children. If government is to pursue policies which influence the way we live together in our families (and given today's realities, that is almost inevitable), it should do so to further, not to frustrate, the basic ties which are the foundations of our civilization.

I believe that this issue can be seen against the background of four areas of governmental policy: attitude toward population growth, education, the role of women, and biological research.

It is obvious that there can be no family unless the propagation of children is present. The Jewish outlook is pro-natalist. The birth of children, where this is possible, is a great blessing. All efforts are expended to make the birth of offspring possible. When children are born, they are welcomed as a gift of God's blessing. The attitude of Judaic tradition is abundantly clear. The attitude of some governmental planners seems to be contrary to the basic outlook of traditional religion.

As an example of the type of government policy which would run counter to the traditional values of the family as outlined in Jewish tradition, let me mention some of the startling points made by Professor Jacqueline Kasun in a recent issue of *The Public Interest* (No. 55, Spring 1979).

Ms. Kasun decided to investigate the type of sex education that was being taught in her own town of Arcata, California. She came up with some surprising and disturbing facts. The curriculum is rather explicit. Seventh and eighth graders are to be taught to "develop an understanding of masturbation." A Planned Parenthood pamphlet recommended by the county health department for use in the local high school says, "If you feel sexy, for heaven's sake admit it to yourself. If the feeling and the tension bother you, you can masturbate. Masturbation cannot hurt you and it will make you feel more relaxed."

High school teachers receive an article in which it is stated, "We must finish the contemporary sex revolution, our society must strive to sanction and support various forms of intimacy between members of the same sex." The sex-curriculum guide for elementary schools specifies that children "will develop an understanding of homosexuality; learn the vocabulary and social fads and engage in role playing about homosexuality."

The type of education pursued brooks no delay. The first grade is treated to a "bathroom tour," accompanied by the naming and explanation of the male and female genital parts.

Professor Kasun describes a class in sexuality which she attended. The teachers distributed instructions for "group drawing of the female and male reproductive organs and

genitals, including the penis, scrotum, testes, vagina, cli-
toris, cervix labia and other parts." The high school students were broken up into groups of four to six persons,
with men and women in each group.

Astonishing figures are cited as to the cost of this type
of sex education. In the spring of 1978 Carter administrative representatives testified before the House Select Committee on Population and suggested an additional 142
million dollars be spent on the federal government's teenage sex-education and birth-control program. Is all this
worth it? In a recent pamphlet "What Parents Should
Know about Sex Education in the Schools," the National
Education Association admits that "while many feel that
sex-education programs are necessary to halt the spread
of venereal disease and the rise in the birth rate of illegiti-
mate children, there is only meager evidence that such
programs reduce the incidence of these phenomena."

What is the ethical basis behind sexuality education?
asks Ms. Kasun. "Stress what is right for the individual,"
advises the curriculum guide for the seventh and eighth
grades. The seventh-grader in Arcata, California, is advised
to set for himself a "purely personal standard of sexual
behavior." Children are urged to make up their own minds,
unburdened of the inhibitions inculcated by religion or
tradition.

The new ethic is based on "responsible sex," i.e., sex
without parenthood. If people insist on having children
they are advised that there are "practical advantages to
the one-child family," including "marital fulfillment,"
"lessened pressures from population growth," and "freedom to organize family activities without conflicts among
children."

While the students are taught to dispel any guilt they
might experience in regard to sexual activity, there is one
anxiety that is stressed: not to add to the population explosion. In a standard pamphlet written by John Burt and

Linda Meeks, fully one quarter of the material is devoted to the population explosion. The pamphlet states that the "explosion is responsible for unemployment, pollution, poverty and starvation." The pamphlet gloomily predicts that unless world population is effectively curbed, average world food intake will decline to mass-starvation levels by the year 2000.

In its publication, *Implementing DHEW Policy on Family Planning* (1966), the Department of Health, Education and Welfare promoted its sex education projects as a means of "effective fertility control . . . especially among minorities."

In surveying the literature used in the classes in sex education, Professor Kasun finds that major emphasis is placed on "population stabilization" and the "effects of overpopulation, crowded housing, lack of farmland, famine and eventual death." The seventh-graders in Humboldt County, California, are instructed in the "permanent methods of birth control: vasectomy and tubal ligation."

Under the guise of providing sex education, the people who promote zero population growth have found an effective outlet to teach their views. They have every right to propagate their ideas. They do not have the right to do so under the public aegis.

Summarizing her disturbing findings, the author concludes, "In undertaking to finance and promote a multimillion dollar program of sex education, the government has entered very heavily into the promotion of a particular world view and the establishment of a chosen ideology, a kind of secular religion." The distinguished columnist George F. Will, reviewing the material presented by Professor Kasun, observes that the sex educators she cites "treat sex as plumbing and partly as recreation. Their's is an American triumph: plumbing for hedonists."

It is obvious that the kind of ideology and outlook on the sexual function which is promoted by the government, at least in this instance, runs counter to all our conceptions about the family, its basis, and its future.

There is a growing feeling in the Jewish community that whatever its virtues and whatever the arguments that can persuasively be marshalled in its behalf, limitation of population presents a treat to Jewish survival. Jewish fertility, current and completed, is about twenty percent less than the Protestant and about twenty-five percent less than the Catholic.[4]

The Jewish tradition, out of both conviction born from consideration of Jewish values, and a sober evaluation of contemporary realities, should be vigorously pro-natalist. It should support those policies of the government which make the bearing and rearing of children economically and socially easier. We might consider such measures as subsidies for families with more than two children, added tax incentives for large families, day care centers for mothers who work or who have no husbands, etc. Thus, the values of Jewish family life can be used as a methodological yardstick to assess governmental policies in sex education, population programs, and family subsidies.

Of equal importance is the issue of *education*. We have seen that in the Judaic viewpoint it is the family—more specifically, the parents—who bear the responsibility for educating their offspring. It has been frequently pointed out that there is a basic difference between the American view of education and the continental view of education. In the American view, the parents are seen as the primary educators. Since the parents cannot themselves manage the complicated enterprise of teaching their offspirng, the state stands *in loco parentis*. It is the agent of the parents in the teaching of the young. In the European view, it is the state that is the primary educator. It prepares children to take their places properly as loyal, informed, and committed citizens. This difference accounts for the fact that

the American polity vests authority for education in local-
ities, while in other countries it is a central ministry of
education which directs the schools and determines their
curricula.

The parents' preference for the type of education their
children should receive (within of course, minimum requirements set by local authority) is, in the American
system, of crucial importance. The parents' concern is
not only for the children's receiving technical and useful information, but also for the inculcation of values
and a world view which will conform with what they
consider best for their children. In the Jewish idiom
this is expressed, as we mentioned previously, in the
parents' responsibility to teach their children Torah.

A derivative of the American viewpoint of these matters is the right of parents to provide alternative modes
of education for their children. Not everyone is expected
or required to send children to the common schools. This
issue was decided in the famous Oregon case which declared, as unconstitutional, requirements which the state
instituted that everyone attend the public schools. Parents who send their children to religiously oriented
schools where values and traditions are taught that are
considered to be vital for the nurture of the young are
not doing anything un-American. They are not under-
mining the common school. They are rather exercising
a basic right that is theirs. The religiously oriented schools
are also providing a very much needed public service: they
are fulfilling the community's duty to provide educational
opportunities for the children of citizens.

If these suppositions are true, then there would be no
good reason why governmental policies which support
private schools—economically, socially and otherwise—
should not be vigorously pursued. The government should,
of course, do everything possible to make all schools edu-

cationally effective. Non-public schools should be included in this assertion of responsibility.

There is, of course, the constitutional question. Does the first amendment to our Constitution bar *any* aid to religiously oriented schools? This question has been debated for decades in various forums, in educational circles, and most importantly in the courts. No clear mandate seems to be evident, though the recent trends seem to be more restrictive than previous ones. It is interesting that in a recent analysis of the debates of the First Congress, which adopted the Bill of Rights, it was shown that the framers of the Constitution did not originally intend to bar aid to *all* religious institutions. Their intention was to bar the establishment of any one particular religion or sect as preferred over all others. This is not the place to enter into the specialized, and often baffling, issue of constitutional law, especially the intriguing question of whether the intention of the framers is crucial in the determination of what *current* law ought to be. However, it is evident, to me at least, that from the point of view of Judaic values and also for the good of the country as a whole, the parents' responsibility for education should be assisted by the government. This would mean support of religiously oriented schools, insofar as this is possible within the parameters of constitutional limitations. In this era of rising inflation, to do less not only thwarts the fulfillment of parental responsibility, but also puts great obstacles in the way of the free exercise of religion, which is provided for in the First Amendment to the Constitution.

It is also evident that government must facilitate the discharge of the parental responsibility to educate their children all along the line. Such government aid must include some form of tax credits for college tuition and the expansion of governmental college tuition loan programs (accompanied by more vigorous means of collection of loans, for the payment of legitimate debts is also a religious duty), etc.

Thus, the pro-natalism of the tradition and the stress on the educational role of the family must be aided and encouraged by governmental policies. The activities of the legislatures and the courts should be evaluated by their conformance to these important values taught by the tradition.

One of the most important developments in contemporary culture has been the emergence of the women's movement. Though some of the views of traditional Judaism have to be modified in order to make it possible for women to participate more fully in the life or our society, it is interesting to note that the commandment requires equal honor and reverence to *father and mother.* Routinely, many feminists condemn the Jewish tradition for subordinating women. Milton Himmelfarb has pointed out an interesting philological fact. The Greek word for womb is *hysteria* as in the surgical procedure hysterectomy, or its psychological derivative hysterical. Hellenically, etymologically at least, the womb generates hysteria. From the Hebrew word for womb, *rehem,* derives *rachamim,* pity, one of the cardinal qualities of God. While philology may prove very little, the Hebraic outlook saw the woman as God's creature, endowed like her male counterpart with the image of God. The liberation of the woman and the opportunities which should be hers to fulfill her intellectual and spiritual needs should not be achieved at the price of removing the woman from her vital function within the family structure.

It is true that a good part of the literature of the woman's liberation movement has been directed against the nuclear family. These attacks have some validity. It is important that women have more in their lives than children and homemaking, if they desire to do so. The novelist Ann Roiphe asserts that the woman's talents and aspirations must be recognized and developed: "If they don't, they wait like a lit hand grenade sitting on the dining room table. In due time the family is certain to blow up."[5] This may be extravagant language, but it does point to a reality present in many homes. It should be possible for women to work, for men to share some of the responsibility for the home, without the family dissolving and without our losing sight of the primary human connections: man, woman, and child. Each one of these factors is important. Yet one function should not be neglected for the sake of the other. We must strive for a society in which equal respect is given to the woman who wants to make pies as to the one who majors in higher mathematics.

Roiphe quotes an anthropologist friend of hers who pointed out that the anti-family feelings, the rise in active homosexual organizations, and the women's liberation movement itself were all part of a cultural collective unconscious move on the part of the species to save itself from the certain ruin of overpopulation. On the face of it, this assertion seems ludicrous. However, there is no doubt that the family is being threatened by attempts to picture the woman's task today as freeing herself from childbearing, by the attempt to have society attest to homosexuality as a viable alternative to traditional life-styles, and by the denigration of the woman who chooses, sometimes defensively and even sheepishly, to devote herself to the nurture of children. These trends threaten not only the existence of the family but the future of the civilization as well.

Women certainly have legitimate complaints against our society. They certainly have the right to demand some modification of ideas about womanhood that have become part of some of our traditional lore. However, these legitimate aspirations can be realized without the destruction of the nuclear family and thereby woman's distinctive quality. Government must be encouraged in its drive to ensure equal rights for women. This hard-won equality is long overdue. However, it should not be achieved at the price of depriving women of their place in the family structure. It must be possible, both practically and socially, for women to fulfill themselves as human beings and to fulfill themselves as women. This means that society as a whole, especially government, must facilitate the pursuit of this double responsibility. Welfare policies, day-care facilities, salary incentives, etc., are all part of the economic enablement of women to take their place in society. The government through its spokesmen plays an important symbolic and cultural role. It must proceed to express its high evaluation of the woman as wife, mother, and grandmother. This it can do by the choice it makes for representatives of the women's movement as well as by economic and other kinds of incentives.

Governmental policies, therefore, in the role of sex discrimination especially as it impinges on the self-image of the woman in our society, should be evaluated by the yardstick which measures the extent to which the woman, no less than the man, while pursuing her legitimate goals, is encouraged to see marriage, the family, and child rearing as a worthy and cherished part of her life.

Another area about which we can speak only briefly is that of governmental policies concerning the funding and encouragement of medical and biological research.

It has been pointed out that our decade and the decades to follow will be recognized as the decades of tremendous progress in biological research. This has led to a cluster of problems and developments which is covered by the term "genetic engineering." The term has never been strictly and precisely defined, and many scientists dislike it intensely.[6] Loosely speaking, it has been used to refer to a wide range of possible and actual scientific breakthroughs such as *in vitro* fertilization, cloning, genetic manipulation, recombinant DNA, and the development of new forms of life. On occasion, prenatal diagnosis is also included.

Judaism has a very positive attitude toward the human right and prerogative to intervene in nature in order to improve the human estate. The biblical assertion that nature is *created* by God, not part of God himself, desanctifies creation. The pagans believed that the gods inhabit nature. The biblical God is above nature. His glory is reflected in nature. The heavens declare the glory of God. They are not God. This means that nature and creation can be exploited and even manipulated for the sake of human betterment. The bold rabbinic assertion is that man can (and indeed is) the partner of God in the creative process. The whole medical enterprise is underpinned by the right of man to challenge that which God has brought about in nature, so to speak. The human being should use his reason, his imagination, and his daring to probe nature and to wrest from it its secrets. This in order to bring healing and health. Of course, we must be prudent in our relationship to nature. We cannot destroy it. We cannot deprive future generations of the benefits of the nature we enjoy. Nature is not sacrosanct—man is. The limit to our manipulative right was defined briefly by Professor James Gustafson:

> A scientist has no right to intervene in the natural processes in such a way that he might alter what men believe to be and value as distinctly human characteristics. A scientist has the right to intervene in the course of human development in such a way that the uses of his knowledge foster growth of those distinctive qualities

of life that humans value most highly; and remove
those qualities that are deleterious and harmful.[7]

These principles mean that we can treat human beings to
improve their humanity; to remove the impediments to
growth, freedom, and intelligence, which are the marks
of the image of God implanted in each one of the human
species. We should not aim to make freedom, intelligence,
and growth impossible.

It is certainly true that being part of a family unit in
which there is a father and a mother, being reproduced
through an act of love of two human beings, is one of
the prime dimensions of human character. To so mecha-
nize reproduction that the function of the family to bear
and nurture children is crucially affected, would not be a
legitimate expression of the human prerogative to intervene in the natural process to produce human happiness.

Spokesmen for the Jewish community have, in general,
hailed the development of *in vitro* fertilization insofar as
it made possible for couples the fulfillment of what is
considered by Hebraic faith as one of the prime responsibilities of the human species: be fruitful and multiply.
The recent event of the birth of the Brown baby was one
of those wonderful expressions of scientific achievement.
Now we are faced with multiple ethical problems. Should
the process of *in vitro* fertilization be extended to single
women? Should research in the creation of artificial en-
vironments which will make human childbearing unneces-
sary be carried on? Should the uncertainties of childbearing be removed by processes which will enable us to determine the sex of the unborn? Should gene therapy be pursued which will remove all possibilities of congenital disease? Should programs of genetic screening be encouraged
which will discourage childbearing on the part of some
and encourage abortions on the part of others? All of

these questions should be evaluated on the basis of whether the distinctive human features which we cherish will be fostered or frustrated by the research which is pursued. Will anonymous and mechanized fertilizations constitute a serious blow to family solidarity and structure? Will the possibilities of childbearing for husbandless women or lesbian couples strengthen the traditional views of the family or weaken them?

Governmental policies play a crucial role in the answer to these and other questions. The government is the prime source of funds for medical and biological research in our country. Whether it funds such research determines whether it will be carried on or not. Recent legislation has established guidelines for certain biomedical processes. We must, as members of the public, be vigilant and concerned that what will help humans become more human, what will assist to eliminate dread diseases and tragic burdens, what will add to the sum total of human happiness—all of these should be encouraged and not frustrated. That which will deprive us of our human stature, which will threaten the family as the basic unit of our civilization, should be, if possible, prevented.

The Judaic view of the family sees the family as indispensable for the future of society. It stresses the blessings of parents and children living and growing together. It asserts the responsibilities for the education of the young to the processes and ideals of our civilization, and asks children to respect, love, and even revere their parents. It hopes both men and women will participate as partners in the education and nurture of the young. If we accept the basic assumptions of Judaic faith, which in large measure are also the basic assumptions of Christian faith, then we have the right and the responsibility to ask that our government help and not hinder the actualization of the values which we literally hold sacred. We ask that the birth of children be encouraged, not disdained; that parents be given the opportunity to educate their children in the light of their own commitments; that the pursuit of the equality of women not be encouraged at the price of removing the honor and dignity of motherhood and the family, and that human ingenuity in relation to nature, which has produced for us so many blessings, will not be carried on to dehumanize us while we exercise our God-given intelligence to probe nature's secrets and even to outwit her when she makes it difficult, if not impossible, to pursue our human goals.

The Hebrew word for man is *ish*, spelled *aleph, yud, shin*. The Hebrew word for woman is *ishah*, spelled *aleph, shin, hey*. The letters which the two words for man and woman have in common are *aleph* and *shin*, which spell the Hebrew word *esh*, fire. The word *ish*, man, has the *yud* not found in *ishah* (woman) and the word *ishah* has the *hey* not found in *ish*. Join *ish* and *ishah*, man and woman, and both have the *yud* and *hey*, which spells *yah*, God. Take away from each that which the other has to offer and what is left is *esh*, fire. Hence, the rabbinic comment that when husband and wife are truly united they express God's presence. When the union is unworthy, it can spell a consuming fire.

This is our choice, as it always has been. Either we will be attached to the divine or we will be consumed.

NOTES

1. Augustine, *City of God,* Book XIX, Chapter XVI.
2. Genesis 2:18–24, E. A. Speiser translation, The Anchor Bible, p. 15.
3. Helmut Thielicke, *The Ethics of Sex,* trans. John W. Doberstein (New York: Harper & Row, 1964), p. 22.

4. Milton Himmelfarb, *Jews of Modernity* (Philadelphia: Jewish Publication Society, 1973), p. 119.

5. Ann Roiphe, "Human drama in a small cage," *New York Times Magazine,* June 26, 1977.

6. Daniel Callahan, "The Moral Career of Genetic Engineering," *The Hastings Center Report,* April 2, 1978.

7. James Gustafson, *The Contributions of Theology to Medical Ethics,* Pere Marquette Lectures (Milwaukee: Marquette University, Theology Department, 1975).

III. Religion and National Economic Policy

Introduction

THE SECOND REPRESENTATIVE issue centers on domestic social policy and the economy.

Rabbi Ben Zion Bokser's paper reflects the Jewish thrust to apply prophetic insights to current economic issues. In this it both illuminates Jewish tradition and illustrates that tradition's passionate struggle to confront conditions of evil. Rabbi Bokser, as a scholar of wide learning actively engaged in the struggle for social justice in the world, is uniquely qualified for this task.

Msgr. George G. Higgins' paper analyzes the development of Catholic understandings of the basic social principles of subsidiarity and voluntary association. As a major proponent of Catholic social action in this country, Higgins' insights into the historical context of the evolution of the concept of *subsidium* ("aid") from *Rerum Novarum* to the present provide an intimate look at the way Catholic social thinkers apply moral principles to the changing needs of society.

Together, the two papers exemplify in microcosm the paradoxically parallel, yet distinct, approaches to social policy of their respective communities. Both papers seek to clarify the traditional stances of their communities on economic issues in general and to probe the ways in which those stances can most effectively be applied to the complex and often intractable issues of the current national debate.

Religion and National Economic Policy: A Jewish Perspective

BEN ZION BOKSER

LIFE IS FRAGMENTED, and the constituent fragments as we encounter them often appear unrelated to each other. But a deep and basic relationship exists, and the fate of any fragment affects the destiny of the whole. The religious life and the political and economic order often appear as separate categories of being. Indeed, it has even been maintained by some that the two realms are wholly apart and sometimes even competitive. According to Marxist economists, religion diverts a person from the economic and political realities and alienates him from coping with the problems of the real world. Similarly, some religionists have looked upon the involvement in worldly concerns as detrimental to spiritual pursuits. From the point of view of Judaism, all life, whatever its manifestation, is a unitary whole. The religious and the economic orders are linked in a basic relatedness. The economic has contributed to the religious, and the religious has vital contributions to make to the economic.

It is clear that man encounters God's providence, in great measure, by experiencing the processes in nature on which he depends for his economic life. He sees God as his shepherd because of whom he is not in want. The abundance that rewards his labors in tilling the soil or tending his flock is only partly the reward of his labors. It is primarily the utilization of resources in nature and in himself which God included in the design of creation. The three major Jewish festivals, Pesach, Shavuot, and Sukkot, have as their primary character the celebration of the harvest, in which God is acknowledged as the source of the sustenance on which man's life depends. The grace after meals offers praise to God "who provides food for each of His creatures." In an industrial society man's labor appears to revolve entirely on man's ordained procedures, in which the element of divine providence is less apparent, but anyone can readily see that in its ultimate character it is similarly based on the utilization of processes, materials, and skills which have their roots in the design of creation. God remains our ultimate Provider.

The design of creation did allow a margin of want among some members of society. Various situational disabilities place some people in the category of the poor. Sometimes these are due to what has occasionally been called "acts of God," but sometimes these are due to human manipulation, in which some, inspired by greed, take command of resources to enlarge their own portion to the detriment of others. The design of creation includes a strategy to cope with this problem. The Bible states lamentably: "Poverty will never cease from the land" (Deut. 15:11). The design of creation includes an element of compassion, which is reinforced by direct exhortations in the revealed teachings of Scripture, to extend help to the needy. When man joins in the rhythm of creation, he emulates God, and "as He is merciful, man is summoned to be merciful." The festivals which celebrate the bounty of harvest include repeated admonitions to share one's substance with the widow, the orphan, and the stranger (Deut. 16:14), and to give to them according to their needs. Where want is experienced as a result of an inequitable or inefficient administration of the resources of nature or of the productive operations, the quality of compassion becomes, in the prophetic figures, in biblical and post-biblical times, a passionate denunciation of injustice and a call to redress the inequities of society to relieve the oppressed and to raise the quality of life of the underprivileged.

Unemployment and inflation are the results of the malfunctioning of our economy, of the technology for the production and distribution of goods and services needed by the people for the sustenance of life. Inflation escalates the cost of living and erodes a person's income, wiping out much of his rewards for hard work, whether in savings or in the funds available to meet ongoing day-to-day needs. Unemployment robs a person of the opportunity to be creative, to enjoy the dignity and independence of earning his daily bread, and, of course, it leaves him, unless society fashions some form of aid to redress his state, in a condition of total deprivation. The pressure on the part of the aggrieved sector of our population, aided by far-sighted and ethically sensitive individuals in other sectors of the population, has resulted in various ameliorative measures to cope with these problems, among them: unemployment insurance, welfare payments to the needy and special provision of aid to families with dependent children, and pensions for retired individuals.

Those sensitive to the prophetic tradition of the Hebrew Bible have often spoken out against the evils this situation represents. But the prophetic sensitivity alone cannot give us the full understanding of the problem and the steps necessary to cope with it. It was Rabbi Kook who distinguished between the prophet whose imaginative faculty stirs him to see the sweep of problems in their most general nature, and the practical person, the technician, who sees the particularities to which a problem is fragmented and the specific remedies through which it may be coped with. The prophet he puts in the category of the poet, and the practical person he designates as the sage. Here are his words:

> As a rule the poets know how to portray the nobler side of life, its beauty, its dynamism and vitality. They also know how to describe the evils of life and to protest against them vigorously. But it is outside the competence of the imaginative faculty to probe the particular conditions that preserve life and safeguard it from even the most minor defects. . . . Here begins the work of physicians, economists, engineers, judges and all those who pursue practical wisdom.[1]

The testimony of economists indicates the full scope of the problem. Unemployment and inflation release forces that generate various other evils that are a major part of the moral decadence of our society. The impact of inflation on the private pensions of retirees has been dramatically described in a Social Security Bulletin published by the U.S. Department of Health, Education, and Welfare: "Inflation has become a serious problem for all Americans, but for those relying heavily on fixed incomes—such as private pensions—the problem is even worse. The consumer price index (CPI) rose 27 percent in the period 1970-74, compared with 5 percent for 1960-64 and 16 percent for 1965-69. It increased an additional 13 percent from 1975 to 1977 and is continuing its steep upward climb in 1978."[2] This in turn has a deleterious effect on the entire family whose resources are continually eroded. The one remedy mentioned is that private pensions emulate the social security arrangement, providing for periodic increases in the pension to correspond to the increases in the cost of living.

Inflation touches, of course, everyone, and most grievously those working for a fixed wage. It releases hardships that touch the entire family and it releases labor unrest exploding occasionally into strikes and violence to adjust wage levels. A healthy society cannot allow runaway inflation. The difficulties of curbing inflation will be less costly than allowing it to proceed on an unchecked momentum.

We have more specific testimony as to the deleterious effects of unemployment. Our society has responded to the deprivation caused by unemployment through the institution of unemployment insurance and welfare payments to the needy. But this does not resolve the problem. Unemployment shatters the morale of the breadwinner. It undermines his dignity. It robs him of hope for the future and creates a climate of stagnation which affects the entire family. It has been shown that "the economic marginality of the father, the lack of necessary monetary resources for proper family functioning and a street scene that is especially attractive to those without external resources" are major factors in family disruption. "This web of factors," the report continues, "produces values and norms that lead to high illegitimacy, marital disruptions and female-headed families."[3] The current practice in payment levels under the program of Aid to Families with Dependent Children favors families headed by women. This has also caused family disruption. The report also testifies: "High welfare payments do help to cause family splitting and do influence women heading families to become welfare recipients."[4] In the light of these facts, the above report submits the following recommendations for change: "Improving wage and employment opportunities of low-income males, or providing the same benefits to two-parent families as to one-parent (female-headed) families; continuing to improve work incentive features in public assistance programs."[5]

The sinister effects of unemployment go beyond the

disruptions of family morale. They inhibit the normal un-
folding of youthful lives. The teenager who sees himself
shut out from productive occupations is thrust into in-
dolence, stagnation, and is often tempted to invest his
unused energies in antisocial ways. The worst effects are
experienced by black teenagers, who are more likely to
be exposed to unemployment. An editorial in the Jesuit
weekly, *America*, underscores the dilemma posed by this
phenomenon:

> Official statistics show that the unemployment rate for
> black teenagers (16–19 years old) has risen from 16.5
> percent in 1954 to 24 percent in 1969, to 36.3 percent
> in 1978. . . . Even more disturbing is the near unanimous
> agreement among observers that the official statistics un-
> derestimate the true extent of black teenage unemploy-
> ment. The consequences of this social dilemma are
> tragic: high crime rates and an ever-growing pool of
> unskilled and disillustioned young men and women.
> Studies indicate that early futility in landing a job has
> deleterious effects on later job performance, only add-
> ing to the bleak prospects this group faces.[6]

The testimonies we have cited are based on the findings
of sociologists and economists, and they indicate that the
sinister effects of inflation and unemployment extend beyond merely monetary deprivation. The Jewish religious
experience reinforces these observations and adds new per-
ceptions based on the theological conception of man's
role in creation. Biblical and talmudic teaching converge
in the perception that man's vocation includes the necessity of being a creative participant in the work of creation.
Even in the Garden of Eden man was assigned a task "to
work it and to watch over it" (Gen. 2:15). According to
some Jewish teachers the commandment, "Six days you
shall work . . . and the seventh day shall be a sabbath
unto the Lord" (Ex. 20:9), involves the duty to work

on the six days as much as it involves the injunction to
rest on the seventh day (Abot de Rabbi Nathan). "Idle-
ness," the Talmud declared, "begets lewdness." Another
view is that it "leads to boredom" (Ketubot 59b). According to this conception even the affluent retiree who
is nonemployed, and not otherwise involved in some
meaningful pursuit, faces a like problem. He violates
a dimension of human nature which bids him be a productive member of society. Inspired by this sensitivity,
we would have to oppose the tendency to compulsory
retirement, regardless of financial arrangement for the
retiree. The right to work is a basic demand of man's
nature, and society should consider it one of the impera-
tives in all strategies of social and economic planning, for
the good of the individual as well as for the good of
society.

Society's responsibility to cope with the problem of
unemployment is illustrated for us in the action of the
Judean authorities in the first century. Josephus describes
a public works project through which the authorities in
Judea sought to deal with a case of unemployment:

> So when the people saw that the workmen were un-
> employed, who were above eighteen thousand, and
> that they, receiving no wages were in want . . . and
> while they were unwilling to keep them by their trea-
> suries that were there [in the Temple] deposited, out
> of fear of their being carried away by the Romans . . .
> so they persuaded him [King Agrippa] to rebuild the
> eastern cloisters. . . . [Agrippa] denied the petitioners
> their request in the matter; but he did not obstruct
> them when they desired the city might be paved with
> white stones. . . .[7]

It is noteworthy that King Agrippa acted under the pressure from the general populace. A high level of moral sensitivity created a general solicitousness for the welfare of

the unemployed, and the pressure of public opinion in-
duced the government authorities to take remedial action.

The erosion of life through the impact of inflation and
unemployment on the individual and the family poses a
challenge for the religiously sensitive person. For the sanctity of life is the highest category of value in the religiously envisioned hierarchy of values. But the challenge
to religion is indeed more direct. Religion is a celebration
of life. On the highest level it is a contemplation of the
mystery of existence, and the mystery which transcends
existence. It is man's rising above his material concerns
to respond to the other dimensions of his nature, the intellectual, the imaginative, the spiritual. But he can only
do this after his basic physical necessities have been relatively met. As Maimonides put it:

> The well-being of the soul comes undoubtedly first in
> rank, but the other, the well-being of the body . . . is
> anterior in nature and time. The latter object is required
> first because the well-being of the soul can only be ob-
> tained after that of the body has been secured; for a
> person that is suffering from great hunger, thirst, heat
> or cold, cannot grasp an idea even if communicated
> by others, much less can he arrive at it by means of
> his own reasoning. But when a person is in possession
> of the first perfection, then he may possibly acquire
> the second perfection, which is undoubtedly of a su-
> perior kind, and is alone the source of eternal life.[8]

The decadence fostered by the social and economic dis-
array as a result of inflation and unemployment, if it is
serious enough, will generate three alternative trends in
the religious life. It will tend, for some people, to make
religion irrelevant in the light of reality and produce a
general disenchantment with it. It will also tend to focus
on low-level religion, one based on fear and rooted in folk
habit and superstitution, functioning in effect, as Marxist

critics have charged, as an opiate of the masses, desensitizing them to their true and intolerable state. But it may
also, in choice individuals, take the form of prophetic criticism of the inequities involved and serve as a force calling
for redress.

The religious community is diverse in its social base.
The challenge of inflation and unemployment emanates
primarily from that sector of society which is immediately
affected by it. But it is precisely this which is the unique
role of religion, that its values are not the rationalization
of class-interest but reflect a sensitivity to the fate of man
as a whole. It represents in its overall character a response
to man's destiny in a world created by God and directed
by His providence. It is understandable that an aggrieved
sector of society will struggle to redress its own conditions. But religion helps translate the need beyond even
proper self-interest. It can transcend it and involve people
who are not in the aggrieved sector—even those in the so-
called privileged sector. Through religion they too may
identify with those who are in need and become involved
prophetically in redressing the evil. Religion must therefore reflect a universality of concern. Nothing that affects
man, whatever his social status, can be alien to it. And
the focus of its concern must be to the measure where
man is most imperiled and the viability of his humanity
is most under challenge. To redress the abuses of our social and economic order must, therefore, be among its
most active concerns.

Religion cannot be the direct agent for social engineering. Religion, to revert to Rabbi Kook's metaphor, being
in the category of the poetic, the imaginative, the prophetic, is enabled to see the general sweep of things, to
call attention to the wrongs encountered, and to disturb
the evading tendency of the complacent who are not
directly affected by those abuses and who would just

as soon leave them unattended. The methodology of redress must come through the initiative of the social technicians, the economists, the sociologists, the legislators. But religion can be and should be the prodding force, the leaven of ferment, the challenge of the conscience, the voice summoning society to cope with the problem.

The force for social change receives its momentum primarily from two sources, from the aggrieved themselves who are stirred to rebel against their lot and from sensitive spirits who are stirred by conscience to strive for equity, who are inspired by love and compassion, who are aware that wrongs unredressed become a festering sore in society, eventually begetting hostility and social breakdown. Religion can play the second role and is uniquely equipped to do so. Its values transcend self-interest and class-interest. It sees all persons as sacred. It sees all persons as endowed with a divine image that needs to be activated to yield moral and ethical sensitivity. Religion has the vision of the ultimate ideal of universal righteousness against which every inequity is an intolerable affront and toward which every inequity redressed is a forward step. Religion needs but to be true to itself to lead in the social effort to overcome the evils that confront us—as in this case, the evils of inflation and unemployment.

NOTES

1. B. Z. Bokser, quoted in *Abraham Isaac Kook*, (New York: Paulist Press, 1978), p. 253.

2. Vol. 41, no. 11, Nov. 1978, p. 16.

3. *Studies on Public Welfare*, published by the Subcommittee on Fiscal Policy, Joint Economic Committee of the U.S. Congress, Paper No. 12 (Part I), p. 20f.

4. Ibid., p. 37.
5. Ibid., p. 38.
6. *America,* March 31, 1979, p. 264f.
7. *Antiquities* XX 9:7.
8. *Guide for the Perplexed,* Part III, Chapter 27.

Religion and National Economic Policy: A Catholic Perspective

GEORGE G. HIGGINS

BY WAY OF INTRODUCTION, it should be noted, if only for background, that the Catholic approach to social and economic problems has undergone a significant change in recent years, more in style, of course, than in substance. At the conscious risk of oversimplication, let me attempt to illustrate this change by reflecting briefly on the contrast between the distinctive style or tone of Pope John XXIII's social encyclicals and that of earlier Church documents on related matters.

Professor E. E. Y. Hales, a British historian who has written extensively on the role of the papacy in the modern world, was one of the first to point out several years ago that Pope John XXIII radically changed the style of official papal documents on socio-economic and political matters. Hales wrote in his excellent biographical study of the late Pontiff:

> John was as anxious as any previous pope to reaffirm some continuity in papal (social) teaching; but in fact, in his brief reign, he changed both its spirit and its content. Still more surprising, he introduced a quite new note of hesitance. . . . It was something new, indeed, when a pope, in an encyclical letter, was prepared

to say this or that was only his personal opinion, using
such phrases as "We consider" or "We maintain" or
"certain factors which seem to have contributed." . . .
Yet doubt where doubt is due, as it is in all questions
of politics and economics, is both intellectually proper
and persuasively effective, and part of the charm of
Pope John was his refusal to pontificate on public
affairs.[1]

Professor Hales' discerning analysis of Pope John's distinctive and highly effective style of teaching in the area
of socio-economic and political problems can be applied
with equal validity to Pope Paul's apostolic letter. That
is to say, the style of the apostolic letter closely parallels
the "persuasively effective" style of Pope John's major
social encyclicals, *Mater et Magistra* and *Pacem in Terris*.
The apostolic letter is written in the form of a familiar
dialogue, not only with Catholics in general, or with Jews
and other believers, but with all men of good will and
carefully avoids the more pontifical style of teaching
which so often characterized similar documents in the
not too distant past.

On some matters, of course, Paul VI states his own
convictions very firmly, but never in such a way as to
force his opinion on the reader or to short-circuit or fore-
close the dialogue. On all matters which are purely contingent and are open legitimately to varying points of
view and lend themselves to a variety of solutions, he
carefully refrains from trying to say—or even leaving the
impression that he is trying to say—the last and final word.
Indeed he goes out of his way to emphasize that it is
neither his ambition nor his mission "to utter a unified
message and to put forward a solution which has universal validity." His purpose is the more modest one of "con-
fiding" his own thoughts and preoccupations about some
of today's more pressing social and economic problems

and of encouraging individual Catholics and groups of Catholics, in dialogue with Jews and other Christians and all men of good will, "to analyze with objectivity the situation which is proper to their own country" and, in addition, "to discern the options and commitments which are called for in order to bring about the social, political, and economic changes seen in many cases to be needed."[2]

Again one is reminded of Pope John's distinctively pastoral style of teaching by Pope Paul's repeated emphasis, in several different contexts, on the legitimate variety or plurality of possible options which are open to men of good will, his related emphasis on the obligation of individual Catholics to form their own conscience on these matters in the light of the Gospel message but without waiting for directives from their ecclesiastical leaders, and, last but not least, his urgent plea for the kind of basic humility which "will rid action of all inflexibility and sectarianism" and for "an effort at mutual understanding of the other's position and motives."

Father M. –D. Chenu, O.P., a distinguished French theologian, who has had a profound influence on a whole generation of younger scholars, has also addressed this subject in a recent book.[3] After quoting at considerable length from the same section of Paul VI's apostolic letter cited by Professor Hales, Father Chenu says that eighty years after Pope Leo XIII's encyclical *Rerum Novarum,* Pope Paul has, in effect, overturned the method or the methodology traditionally followed in official Church documents on social issues. That method, he says, is now more inductive than deductive and puts more emphasis on pluralism. This emphasis, Chenu continues, is not only a response to the diversity of situations in which Christians find themselves in today's world, it derives from the very nature of the Church's renewed understanding of her mission in the world as outlined, for example, in several of the major documents of Vatican II.

In summary, Chenu says that we no longer speak of Catholic social "doctrine," but rather of Catholic social teaching or the social teaching of the Gospel. In this connection, he cites the full text of paragraph 42 of *Octogesima Adveniens,* which reads as follows:

> In the face of so many new questions the Church makes an effort to reflect in order to give an answer, in its own sphere, to men's expectations. If today the problems seem original in their breadth and their urgency, is man without the means of solving them? It is with all its dynamism that the social teaching of the Church accompanies men in their search. If it does not intervene to authenticate a given structure or to propose a ready-made model, it does not thereby limit itself to recalling general principles. It develops through reflection applied to the changing situations of this world, under the driving force of the Gospel as the source of renewal when its message is accepted in its totality and with all its demands. It also develops with the sensitivity proper to the Church which is characterized by a disinterested will to serve and by attention to the poorest.
>
> Finally, it draws upon its rich experience of many centuries which enables it, while continuing its permanent preoccupations, to undertake the daring and creative innovations which the present state of the world requires.[4]

According the Chenu, the significance of the Church's new approach to social and economic problems, as illustrated by the encyclicals of John XXIII and Paul VI's apostolic letter, is that the Church is now in less danger of canonizing any particular historical system or any particular status quo.

Father Yves Congar, O.P., one of Chenu's most distinguished disciples, makes substantially the same point in a recent essay entitled, in loose translation from the French, "Is There Such a Thing as Catholic Social Doctrine?" Yes, he says, but it is necessary to be very precise about the meaning of the term. He points out that Vatican II's Pastoral Constitution on the Church in the Modern World deliberately avoided using the term because of its ambiguity. It could mistakenly be understood, for example, as a body of settled doctrine or dogma or even as a complete program of political action. It is not that, he says. To the contrary, it has an open and dynamic character. While it lays down certain general principles, the application of these principles varies with different conditions and circumstances.

This is not to say, however, that Catholic teaching on social matters is purely relativistic or of no practical importance. There is, in fact, a substantial body of such teaching—teaching of a very practical nature—on the fundamental rights of the human person as a responsible social being.

Perhaps the most concise listing of these basic human rights is to be found in Pope John XXIII's encyclical *Pacem in Terris*. There is no need at this time to run through this list. Suffice it to note that *Pacem in Terris,* like numerous other Church documents on this general subject, lays great emphasis on the right of men and women to found a family, "the first and essential cell of society." From this it follows, the encyclical says, "that most careful provision must be made for the family both in economic and social matters as well as in those which are of a cultural and moral nature," all of which look to the strengthening of the family and helping it carry out its function.

Later in the same document, we read that

Individual citizens and intermediate groups are obliged to make their specific contributions to the common welfare. One of the chief consequences of this is that they must bring their own interests into harmony with the needs of the community, and must contribute their goods and their services as civil authorities have prescribed, in accord with the norms of justice and within the limits of their competence. Clearly then those who wield power in the state must do this by such acts which not only have been justly carried out, but which also either have the common welfare primarily in view or which can lead to it.

Indeed since the whole reason for the existence of civil authorities is the realization of the common good, it is clearly necessary that, in pursuing this objective, they should respect its essential elements, and at the same time conform their laws to the circumstances of the day.[5]

And again, with more direct reference to the subject of dialogue, *Pacem in Terris* speaks very clearly about the duty of civil authorities to bring about a situation in which individual citizens and intermediate groups can easily exercise their rights and fulfill their duties as well:

For experience has taught us that, unless these authorities take suitable action with regard to economic, political and cultural matters, inequalities between the citizens tend to become more and more widespread, especially in the modern world, and as a result human rights are rendered totally ineffective and the fulfillment of duties is compromised.

It is therefore necessary that the administration give wholehearted and careful attention to the social as well as to the economic progress of the citizens, and to the development, in keeping with the development of the productive system, of such essential services as the building of roads, transportation, communications, water supply, housing, public health, education, facilitation of the practice of religion, and recreational facilities. It is necessary also that governments make efforts to see that insurance systems are made available to the citizens, so that, in case of misfortune or increased family responsibilities, no person will be without the necessary means to maintain a decent standard of living. The government should make similarly effective efforts to see that those who are able to work can find employment in keeping with their aptitudes, and that each worker receives a wage in keeping with laws of justice and equity. It should be equally the concern of civil authorities to ensure that workers be allowed their proper responsibility in the work undertaken in industrial organization, and to facilitate the establishment of intermediate groups which will make social life richer and more effective. Finally, it should be possible for all citizens to share as far as they are able in their country's cultural advantages.[6]

I take it that very few people in our society would openly disagree with any of these statements as a matter of principle—or, for that matter, with similar statements on the subject of human rights in the U.S. Declaration on Human Rights, for example, or in any of the numerous documents on human rights issued by Jewish and Protestant agencies. The problem arises when some of the specific rights listed in these documents are—or, in any event, are made to appear to be—in conflict with one another. This real or alleged conflict between competing human rights obviously has a distinct bearing on the subject we are discussing in this dialogue.

Father David Hollenbach, S.J., of the Woodstock Theological Center in Washington, D.C., has recently published a scholarly study devoted explicitly to this matter. His book is entitled *Claims in Conflict: Retrieving and Renewing the Catholic Human Rights Tradition.* "Fundamental to this debate [over the conflict of rights]," he writes, "is a disagreement about how different social agents can and should be interrelated. Efforts to defend human rights must necessarily assign relative weights to the activity and power of individual persons, to the action of the whole society organized by government, and to the action of intermediate groups such as families, local communities, labor unions, professional associations, etc. Disputes about conflicting rights claims are frequently rooted in disagreement about the relative social importance and capabilities of these diverse groups."

"In modern Catholic social thought," Father Hollenbach continues, "this issue has been addressed by appealing to the 'principle of subsidiarity.' Some form of this principle can be found in nearly every major social document of the tradition since *Rerum Novarum*. It was given its classic formulation by Pius XI in *Quadragesimo Anno*:

> Just as it is wrong to take away from individuals what by their own ability and effort they can accomplish and commit it to the community, so it is an injury and at the same time both a serious evil and a perturbation of the right order to assign to a larger and higher society what can be performed successfully by smaller and lower communities. This is a fixed and unchangeable principle most basic in social philosophy, immovable and unalterable. The reason is that all social activity, of its very power and nature, should supply help to the members of the social body, but may never destroy or absorb them.

"The principle states that government intervention is justified when it truly provides help ('*subsidium*') to the persons and smaller communities which compose society. More importantly, however, the family, the neighborhood, the church, and both professional and labor groups all have a dynamic life of their own which must be respected by government. There are legitimate claims rooted in the dynamics and structure of these groups."[7]

Let me now elaborate on this principle, the principle of subsidiarity, in terms of our own Catholic experience in the United States, with at least indirect reference to the subject of unemployment and inflation as these twin evils affect the family in our society.

Let me try to put this problem in historical perspective, starting with a brief reference to several recent developments which have a distinct bearing on the subject under discussion.

The 1976 Wanderer Forum, in a resolution on political action, called upon the Church to keep in mind the principle of subsidiarity. According to the resolution, subsidiarity dictates that social and political action be taken at the lowest and most decentralized level possible.

Concurrently, Father Andrew Greeley, in two of his recent books, and Jesuit Father John Coleman of the School of Theology at Berkeley, in a recent article in *America*, have also emphasized the importance of this principle and have criticized the current breed of Catholic social actionists for failing, allegedly, to be guided by it in their own approach to social and economic reform. Father Coleman says, for example, "for most of the post-Vatican II Church, it is as if that tradition never existed or were totally corrupt."

Dr. Peter Berger, sociology professor at Rutgers University, and Rev. Richard J. Neuhaus, a Lutheran inner-city pastor in Brooklyn and senior editor of *Worldview*, have also concurrently launched an extensive study program aimed at strengthening what they call "intermediate structures"—all of those voluntary structures (the family, church-related, and other voluntary social agencies, etc.) which stand between the individual and the state. Berger and Neuhaus fully understand, of course, that the state has an indispensable role to play in meeting human needs and that the philosophy of laissez-faire is as dead as a dodo. They are pleased that the problems that used to be attributed to individual laziness, the will of God, or just bad luck, have belatedly become the object of social policy. In other words, their study project is not aimed at dismantling the so-called welfare state as such.

On the other hand, as Neuhaus points out in a recent book: "Only in recent years have those who cared deeply about the plight of the poor begun to reexamine the linkage between social responsibility and state implementation. . . . What is at stake in this question touches upon the very heart of American pluralism. . . . While the state necessarily has the sole power to taxation, there is no necessity about its having the sole or even primary role in meeting the human needs for which such taxes are raised. Other approaches must be explored before the self-aggrandizing bureaucracy of government . . . precludes alternatives."[8]

Father Greeley, for his part, has complained in a recent column that Berger and Neuhaus have propounded the traditional Catholic principle of subsidiarity without a single mention of Jacques Maritain, Yves Simon, John Courtney Murray, John Ryan, Pius XI, or Thomas Aquinas. Whatever of that, the fact that the principle of subsidiarity is simultaneously being emphasized by people as far apart in their thinking as the delegates to the Wanderer Forum, on the one hand, and Greeley, Coleman, Berger, and Neuhaus, on the other, is not surprising. As Greeley has pointed out, "Opposition to big government is no longer a predictor of a right-wing stance on any other issue . . . [and] support of big government is no longer a predictor of a left-wing stance either."[9] His point was borne out in the 1976 political campaign, with candidates of all shades arguing that "small is beautiful," the title of an influential book by the late E. F. Schumacher.

I am glad that this point is being made so effectively by Catholic and non-Catholic scholars and by politicians as well. On the other hand, a word of caution is in order. To say that "small is beautiful" is not to say, without a carload of qualifications, that that government is best which governs least or that so-called big government is by definition a violation of the principle of subsidiarity.

Pursuing this point, let me now jump back to an earlier period in American history. One hundred fifty-three years have elapsed since Alexis de Tocqueville wrote his celebrated and still widely quoted essay titled "Of the Use Which the Americans Make of Public Associations in Civil Life." By "public associations" he meant "only those associations that are formed in civil life without reference to political objectives." He noted with satisfaction and thought it very praiseworthy that "Americans of all ages, all conditions, and all dispositions continually form associations . . . not only commercial and manufacturing companies . . . but associations of a thousand other kinds, religious, moral, serious, futile, general or restricted, enormous or diminutive. . . . Thus the most democratic country on the face of the earth is that in which men have, in our time, carried to the highest perfection the art of pursuing in common the object of their common desires and have applied this new science to the greatest number of purposes."[10]

De Tocqueville thought that there was a necessary connection between the principle of association and that of equality. "Among the laws that rule human societies," he concluded, "there is one which seems to be more precise and clear than all others: If men are to remain civilized or to become so, the art of associating together must grow and improve in the same ratio in which the equality of conditions is increased."[11]

De Tocqueville's idealization of voluntary institutions

or associations—including private charitable, philanthropic, and mutual-aid societies—served to remind his readers in this country as well as in Europe that—perennial American rhetoric to the contrary notwithstanding—voluntary association, rather than "individualism," was the real key to an understanding of the American social system. I think it would be fair to say that in the 1830s and for the rest of the nineteenth century most Americans would have agreed with de Tocqueville that voluntary association was a dynamic, progressive influence in American life. As Dr. Roy Lubove, associate professor of social welfare at the University of Pittsburgh, pointed out a decade ago, prior to the twentieth century voluntary association "not only played a mediating role between the individual and society, but made limited government possible by diffusing power and responding to collective needs."

By the turn of the century, however, Professor Lubove continues,

the ideology of voluntarism and the vast network of institutional interests which it had nurtured had become retrogressive in many respects. Assumptions about the self-sufficiency and superiority of voluntary institutions obstructed adaptation to changing economic and social conditions. And nowhere did the rigidities of the voluntary creed prove more disastrous than in the area of social welfare legislation, as demonstrated by efforts to enact a comprehensive economic security program before the 1930s. In other areas as well—low-cost housing, medical care and urban planning—voluntarism became, as I. M. Rubinow put it, the great American substitute for social action and policy. What occurred was the creation of socio-economic no-man's-lands; voluntary institutions failed to respond to mass needs, but thwarted governmental efforts to do so.[12]

If de Tocqueville was the most celebrated proponent

of voluntary association in the nineteenth century, Dr. Rubinow, who did so much to promote the cause of social insurance in this country, was one of its most persistent critics during the first three decades of the twentieth century. Rubinow's criticism, which was often acerbic and sarcastic in tone, was directed quite specifically at the social work profession. In the words of Professor Lubove, Rubinow "felt that social workers held many conventional views on the relation between voluntary institutions, economic incentives, and the preservation of moral standards. . . . Their criticisms of public assistance, and obsession with individual responsibility for protection against economic adversity, provoked Rubinow. . . . Many social workers [he felt] did not recognize that economic security was necessarily the responsibility of the public welfare sector. As [he] argued until the Depression of the 1930s proved him correct, private social work lacked the resources. . . . Private social work (he bitterly complained) was indifferent or opposed to extension of public assistance programs, but professional social workers had lost interest in the relief of destitution."

For his own part, Professor Lubove agrees in substance with Rubinow on the matter under discussion.

The efforts of social workers, psychiatrists, and others to increase scientific understanding of personality were legitimate, but the pendulum had swung too far. The helping professions had forgotten how much the individual remained "subject to the conditions of social organization." Equally pertinent, the concept of poverty was changing. In "dynamic industrial societies" any definition of poverty had to be based upon "comparative scales and standards of living." The need for social insurance and assistance programs increased rather than diminished as living standards rose. Private, voluntary institutions and casework could not cope with poverty in the older, static sense of inability to obtain "those necessities which will permit . . . a state of physical efficiency." The new, dynamic definition would require an even greater redistributive effort, one based upon the resources and coercive powers of the state.[13]

I have cited Dr. Rubinow and Professor Lubove so extensively in this context simply to suggest that the problem which they have raised—namely, the inherent limitations of remedial social work and the relationship between state and private agencies—is one which must be constantly reexamined in the light of rapidly changing social, economic, and political conditions in the United States.

At this point it may be appropriate to say a few words about Msgr. William Kerby's book, *Social Mission of Charity*,[14] with special reference to some of Kerby's observations on justice, charity, equality, and property. Kerby had a profound influence on the development of the Catholic social action movement in the United States.

I should like to say at the outset that Kerby's book, however conservative it may appear to be by the standards of 1979, was reasonably progressive by the standards of 1921. There is no record of what Dr. Rubinow thought about the book, but I suspect that even he, for all of his transplanted and watered-down socialist convictions, might have found it at least partially to his liking. I say this because Kerby, while giving due attention and attaching due importance to remedial social welfare under voluntary auspices, repeatedly called upon the social work profession to take an organic view of poverty and relief and to engage in social action to eliminate the institutional causes of poverty. By temperament and training, Kerby was less "radical," if you will, than his contemporary, Msgr. John A. Ryan. Nevertheless, his emphasis on a preventive, as opposed to a purely remedial, approach to poverty and his related emphasis on the need for governmental action to eliminate the causes of poverty was in the Ryan tradition and has left its mark on the American Catholic social action movement.

We can only guess what Kerby would have written about justice, charity, equality, and property if he had lived to witness the Great Depression, World War II, the Korean conflict, and the war in Vietnam, to say nothing of the current crisis in the field of race relations and urban affairs.

In any event, I like to think that, while holding fast to the principle of subsidiarity and the principle of voluntary association, he would have welcomed the more flexible—and, if you will, more "liberal"—application of these principles which we find, for example, in the encyclical *Mater et Magistra* and in the writings of so many contemporary social thinkers. In Kerby's day, even "mature liberals" in the field of health and welfare were somewhat inclined to interpret the principle of subsidiarity to mean that that government is best which governs least. I am not suggesting, of course, that Kerby himself subscribed to this point of view. I am merely saying, as previously noted, that there was a tendency in his day to be more wary of government intervention in the socio-economic order than most of us tend to be at the present time.

Be that as it may, the principle of subsidiarity, as we understand it today, does not mean that that government is best which governs least. On the contrary it means that, while government should not arbitrarily usurp the role of individuals or voluntary organizations in social and economic life, neither should it hesitate to adopt such programs as are required by the common good and are beyond the competence of individual citizens or groups of citizens.

There is no imprecision, no qualification like "as much as possible," or "as little as possible," in the principle of the state's subsidiarity relationship to lesser societies. The way in which things fall out is somewhat as follows: The state can and ought of itself to perform its proper functions for the general and universal common good and for the realization of distributive justice; it will perform these duties, among others, by giving aid to other societies to the extent that they would otherwise not be able to solve the problems which normally belong to them. But it must take care that, while doing this, it also does its own task. Its subsidiary role with regard to lesser societies and individuals is not subsidiary by reference to the state itself, nor to the nature of society as a whole. Still less must "subsidiary" be taken to imply secondary, and the state itself thought of as such. *Subsidium* means aid, help. The state brings aid and help. The principle of subsidiarity is concerned with the relationship of the state to other societies, not with the nature of the state itself.

Certain Catholic writers may themselves be partially to blame that so many non-Catholics fail to see that this is the real meaning of the principle of subsidiarity in the Catholic tradition of social ethics. Some Catholic writers, in an effort to highlight the importance of voluntary, non-governmental organizations, may have left the impression, inadvertently, that they were playing down the proper role of government in the field of social welfare and economic reform.

If any Catholic writers in the past have taken such a one-sided view of the principle of subsidiarity, they will want to redress the balance in the light of Pope John XXIII's two great encyclicals, *Mater et Magistra* (Christianity and Social Progress) and *Pacem in Terris* (Peace on Earth).

One of the most noteworthy features of these two

encyclicals is their realistic and highly sophisticated emphasis on the need for government to play an increasingly more important role in social life because of the complexity of the problems that have arisen since the publication of Leo XIII's *Rerum Novarum* and Pius XI's *Quadragesimo Anno* (1931).

Leo XIII, in the former document, tended by and large to treat the role of government in a rather gingerly or cautious manner—and quite understandably so. He was looking over his shoulder at a very doctrinaire type of European socialism.

Forty years later, Pius XI was able to take a slightly more relaxed approach to the role of government in social and economic life. He laid great stress on the importance of governmental action as one means—though not the only means, of course—of solving the social and economic problems of the 1930s. On balance, however, both Leo XIII and Pius XI tended to approach the role of government in socio-economic life with a certain amount of caution and reserve.

The importance of the more recent encyclicals is that their author, Pope John XXIII, was able to take a somewhat more relaxed view with regard to the role of government in social and economic life. He took the position that the problems which have arisen in the past forty or fifty years have become so complex that there must be the closest possible cooperation between voluntary groups and the government and that the government, in addition to helping voluntary groups, wherever feasible, is also required to do more, on its own initiative, in the field of social welfare and social reform.

Pope John XXIII's forward-looking treatment of the role of government in social and economic life is very timely. We Catholics have justifiably prided ourselves on having helped to keep alive the notion of subsidiarity in social and economic life. But if we are going to be faithful to the spirit as well as the letter of Catholic social teaching, we must now be equally alive to the importance and indispensability of far-reaching governmental action in the social and economic order.

Take the case of poverty, for example. There is much that individual citizens and groups of citizens can do to alleviate this problem, but they cannot solve the problem alone. The government will have to do much more than it is doing at the present time and probably more than any recent administration has proposed.

The principle of subsidiarity, properly understood, does not prohibit the government from meeting this pressing challenge. On the contrary, it obliges the government to supplement the necessarily limited programs of voluntary organizations in the field of social welfare and social reform.

It is very important to keep this principle alive at a time when so many people are being tempted to go overboard on Proposition 13 and allied proposals. This is not the appropriate forum in which to analyze this ambiguous phenomenon in detail. For present purposes, suffice it to say that, in my opinion, simplistic support of the philosophy underlying Proposition 13 runs counter to the social philosophy of our organizations and could prove to be disastrous to many of our clients. I realize, of course, that many economists disagree with me in this regard. Professor Arthur Burns, for example, is of the opinion that essential services will not be cut as a result of Proposition 13. "I think," he said at a recent forum in Washington, D.C., "local governments will act more or less rationally in adjusting to the smaller amount of money that is available for expenditure." Significantly, however, he added with becoming modesty: "I can't be sure of that." Indeed he can't.

I do not share Dr. Burns' easy optimism about the impact of Proposition 13. I am more inclined to share the qualified pessimism of Walter Heller, former chairman of the Council of Economic Advisers, who told the same Washington forum:

> I am extremely dubious. When you knock $7 billion out of the $12 billion local property tax, it is going to take the wisdom of Solomon to allocate that cutback in an efficient and fair manner. I am also afraid that I can't interpret this California vote as people grabbing control of their own destiny. It was a blind, self-interest-motivated lashing out at government. Now, whenever one makes a statement like that one has to go on and say there were some genuine grievances, but simply to say, "I want to lower taxes for myself," is not my idea of a national crusade for reestablishing one's own destiny. That certainly applies as well to putting a provision into the state constitution requiring a two-thirds vote of both houses of the state legislature to enact any new taxes to take the place of the old.

As Msgr. John A. Ryan told the Minnesota State Conference of Charities way back in 1912, "only the state can prevent a large part, probably the larger part, of the social distress which is due primarily to environment." Needless to add, Dr. Ryan also noted on this occasion that while "the sphere of the state in dealing with social distress is by no means small, neither is it indefinitely large. It is confined within fairly definite limits by certain clear and fundamental principles. Neither in the field of prevention nor in that of relief is it wise or right for the state to do anything that can be done as well by voluntary agencies; and wherever practicable, it should subsidize, cooperate with and supplement private effort." Eight years later, Dr. Ryan returned to the latter point in a lecture delivered at commencement exercises of the New York School of Social Work:

> According to the Catholic view the question whether state funds devoted to the relief of the distressed and to the care of dependents should be administered by the state, or by private agencies, is entirely one of expediency. There is no question here of principle. If a private agency can administer state funds, always under adequate state supervision, in such a way as to produce a greater amount of more beneficial service, that is the better arrangement. Moreover, there are special reasons for desiring that dependents, especially young dependents, should be cared for in Catholic rather than in state institutions; namely, the necessity of giving them adequate training in religion and religious morality. If this can be done with the aid of state money in Catholic institutions so as to produce better social and civic results than would be obtained through the same expenditure of state money in state institutions, there can be no possible doubt that this arrangement is preferable.

Father Bernard Coughlin has developed the latter point in greater detail in his book, *Church and State in Social Welfare.* "It is not a question," Coughlin points out in his concluding chapter, "of government versus voluntary welfare, as the problem was frequently stated in the 1930s. Every social means, if rightly used, can be an instrument for good. The problem is the right use of both government and voluntary welfare, and this requires a public policy that will assure government responsibility where necessary and a sister policy that will counterbalance government responsibility where necessary and a sister policy that will counterbalance government responsibility."[15]

This two-pronged emphasis on the need for extensive

state action on the one hand and, on the other hand, the need for a proper division of labor and closer cooperation between state and private agencies was strongly echoed in Dr. Kerby's book, *The Social Mission of Charity.* Moreover, it has always found favor in the Catholic social action movement.

In passing, it is well to note that Msgr. Paul Hanly Furfey, in his most recent book, *Love and the Urban Ghetto,* pointedly suggests that there is a basic flaw in the philosophy of Catholic liberalism which, in his opinion, has been the underlying philosophy of the Catholic social action movement in general:

> It would be grossly unfair to minimize the good effects of the movement here called Catholic liberalism. It has encouraged the passage of good social legislation. . . . Working conditions have been enormously improved over the last century. And most certainly, social work, including Catholic social work, has helped the poor in many ways. . . .
> Yet liberalism has obviously failed to solve the central problem considered in this book, the agony of those 25 million poor in this most affluent land. Liberalism has indeed helped reduce the number of the poor, yet that number remains large to a ghastly degree.[16]

Msgr. Furfey goes on to cite still another problem. He says that "only a few of those who help the poor actually help them face-to-face. . . . Most middle-class people comfortably assume that the poor are adequately taken care of by the various forms of welfare without having any idea of how cruelly low welfare payments actually are. This ignorance is comfortable. What we don't know doesn't upset us. Liberalism lulls the conscience of the middle class."

Msgr. Furfey's point is well taken and he of all people has the right to make it so bluntly, for throughout his

entire lifetime he has consistently lived up to his forbid-
dingly high standards in this regard. I am not disposed,
then, even to comment on his forceful statement about
the limits of what he calls Christian liberalism. Far better
simply to pray about it in a spirit of humility.

My purpose in spending so much time elaborating on
the meaning, within our own American Catholic experience, of the principle of subsidiarity is to suggest that
there is no easy or simplistic answer—from the point of
view of social ethics or, more specifically, from the point
of view of Catholic social teaching—to the twin problem
of unemployment and inflation or to any of the other
complex economic problems confronting our nation and
indeed the entire world at the present time. My own organization, as you will note from reading almost any collection of statements and background papers we have
issued over the years, favors a high degree of governmental intervention to solve the problem of unemployment.
For example, it supports the Humphrey-Hawkins Full
Employment Act. I concur with this endorsement, but
I fully realize—and I am sure my colleagues who drafted
our position papers on this matter also fully realize—that
reasonable people may legitimately favor other options.
From the point of view of sound social ethics, however,
it seems to me that there can be little room for disagreement with the position taken by our Conference and by
all of the major religious groups in the United States that
full employment is a compelling ethical imperative and
that solving the problem of inflation by creating high
levels of unemployment runs contrary to the dictates of
social justice.

While the nation continues to grapple with the respective roles of government and private enterprise in resolving these two problems and a number of related problems
confronting the American economy, let me add a personal

word of caution about the danger of neglecting another basic principle in the corpus of Catholic social teaching, namely the right of workers to organize for the purpose of collective bargaining and, beyond that, the need to encourage and enable workers to exercise this basic right. While I favor whatever degree of governmental intervention which may be necessary to provide a decent minimum of economic security for American families, I am convinced that, over the long haul, governmental action in this and related areas is no substitute for a strong and effective labor movement.

And yet, if I am not mistaken, the religiously oriented social action movement in this country has shown less interest in the trade union problem in recent years than it did a generation ago. I have the impression, however, that the tide may be turning again, this time in what I would consider to be the right direction.

During the first half of this century—and particularly during the 30s and 40s—the Catholic social action movement in the United States gave special attention to the problem of labor-management relations. It was concerned first and foremost with defending the right of workers to organize into unions of their own choice and took the position that, as a general rule, there is a certain moral obligation to join a union whenever circumstances clearly require workers to organize in defense of their legitimate economic interests.

After the Second World War there was a gradual tapering off of direct involvement by Catholic social actionists in the field of labor-management relations, as concerned priests, religious, and lay leaders began to concentrate on a number of other social and economic problems which were thought to be of greater urgency. All things considered, that was a normal and natural development designed to meet the changing needs of changing times. To some extent, however, it may have been based on the mistaken notion that the labor problem has become a dead issue or, in any event, that the basic right of workers to organize is no longer in dispute.

It is now clearly evident that such is not the case. Despite the progress of recent decades, the right of workers to organize is still a very live issue. The right itself, of course, is seldom, if ever, explicitly or directly challenged as a matter of theory, but, in practice, hundreds of thousands of workers are still struggling against very difficult odds to achieve the protection and benefits of collective bargaining long since enjoyed by their fellow workers in most of the basic industries in the United States.

It is for this reason that, in recent years, there has been a revival of interest in the problem of labor-management relations on the part of the Catholic social action movement, with an ever increasing number of Catholic leaders and Catholic organizations coming to the support of unorganized farm workers in the Southwest and textile workers in the Southeastern part of the country, to cite but two examples.

In doing so, they have the full support of Pope John Paul II, who, in the last of the major addresses which he delivered during his recent visit to Mexico, dealt specifically with the problems faced by working men and women in today's rapidly changing world. Standing on a bridge overlooking the city of Monterrey, which is to Mexico what Pittsburgh is to the United States, he spoke with great feeling, in the light of his own earlier experience in Poland as a factory worker, about "the need for work that suits the lofty dignity of man" and is not a cause of alienation and frustration. "I cannot forget," he continued, "the difficult moments during the world war when I had the direct experience of physical work . . . , of the fatigue, the dependence it imposes, the stress and monotony of it. I have shared the needs of working men and women, their just demands and legitimate aspirations."

Working men and women, His Holiness said, aspire "to more human conditions, to greater security, to a fairer participation in the fruits of their common labor regarding wages, social security and opportunities for cultural and spiritual growth. They want to be treated as free and responsible men and women, able to participate in the decisions which affect their life and their future. It is a fundamental right of workers to freely establish organizations to defend and promote their interests and to contribute in a responsible manner to the common good."[17]

NOTES

1. E. E. Y. Hales, *Pope John and His Revolution* (London: Eyre and Spottswoode, 1968), p. 28.

2. Pope Paul VI, apostolic letter *Octogesima Adveniens* (A Call to Action) (USCC edition, 1971), p. 3.

3. M. -D. Chenu, O.P., *The Social Doctrine of the Church: Its Origins and Development, 1891-1971* (published in Italian and French, but not yet available in English).

4. Pope Paul VI, *Octogesima Adveniens*, p. 42.

5. Pope John XXIII, *Pacem in Terris* (USCC edition, 1963).

6. Ibid.

7. David Hollenbach, S.J., *Claims in Conflict: Retrieving and Renewing the Catholic Human Rights Tradition* (New York: Press, 1979), pp. 156-157.

8. Richard Neuhaus, *Time Toward Home: The American Experiment as Revelation* (New York: Seabury Press, 1975).

9. Andrew M. Greeley, *The Communal Catholic* (New York: Seabury Press, 1976), p. 101.

10. De Tocqueville, *Democracy in America*, Vol. II, Second Book, Chapter V.

11. Ibid.

12. Roy Lubove, *The Struggle for Social Security, 1900-1935* (Cambridge, Mass.: Harvard University, 1968).

13. Ibid.

14. William Kerby, *Social Mission of Charity* (1921).

15. Bernard Coughlin, *Church and State in Social Welfare*, (New York: Columbia University Press, 1965), p. 135.

16. Paul H. Furfey, *Love and the Urban Ghetto*, (Maryknoll, N.Y.: Orbis Books, 1978).

17. Pope John Paul II, address, Monterrey, Mexico. *Origins* 8 (NC Documentary Service), (Feb. 15, 1979), p. 556.

IV. Religion and International Human Rights

Introduction

THE CASE STUDY question posed in this section is how the religious community can confront violations of human rights that exist in other nations of the world.

Father Hehir's incisive paper utilizes the tools of the political scientist to analyze the Church's role as a transnational actor on the world scene. Because of its international ties, he notes, the local Church is often the sole institution in a given country that cannot be shut down by dictatorships. This often gives it a unique opportunity and responsibility for championing human rights within repressive societies.

Catholic theory, Father Hehir pointed out in discussion, is grappling today with the question of whether there exist moral absolutes. While positive *dicta* cannot easily be absolutized, are there certain acts in war, such as the saturation fire-bombing of civilian targets, which are *never* permissible morally?

While most international questions, including human rights, involve situations where values are in conflict, there are some cases, Professor Wyschogrod states, where the evil involved is so awesome as to pose an absolute imperative for religious action that cuts through all normal moral balancing. For Wyschogrod, the Holocaust provides a paradigm for such a category of "abnormal evil" which can only be met by the unambiguous, prophetic voice and direct intervention even in the internal affairs of the offending nation. Had Hitler not invaded Poland, would the allies still have been justified in declaring war? What should have been our response to other genocidal outrages, for example in Uganda and Cambodia?

Religion and International Human Rights: A Catholic Perspective

J. BRYAN HEHIR

THE ASSIGNED TOPIC OF this paper is "How We Confront Violations of Basic Human Rights in International Policy." The instructions which accompanied the assignment emphasized the need to concentrate on methodological questions in each of our traditions. To fulfill this mandate, I have divided the presentation into three topics: (1) Catholic moral theory and human rights; (2) Catholic ecclesiology and human rights; (3) Catholic organizational polity and human rights.

I. Catholic Moral Theory and Human Rights

For a religious institution to confront human rights violations in the international arena, it is necessary for it to have a functioning theory of rights. Such a theory is necessarily a work of politico-moral analysis which defines the meaning of human rights, identifies the spectrum of rights acknowledged in the theory, and relates the religious vision of human rights to the wider secular debate. In Catholic theology the dominant mode of moral discourse concerning human rights has been the natural law tradition.

It is not possible within the limits of this presentation to articulate the philosophical argument which sustains the natural law ethic. It is even less feasible to enumerate the philosophical and theological critiques of natural law which challenge this mode of argument today. All that is possible here is to identify the fact that Catholic teaching on human rights has been permeated by natural law philosophy and then to indicate the principal characteristics of a natural law exposition of human rights claims.

In terms of social policy, the best description of the natural law ethic is John Courtney Murray's remark that natural law represents the tradition of reason in public affairs. The meaning of this statement is made more explicit by Father Charles Curran's explanation that Catholic teaching on natural law affirms a second source of a moral wisdom, derived from reason, which complements what we learn from the revealed word of the Scriptures.[1]

Curran, following Maritain, argues that this second source of moral wisdom is structured in terms of two questions: the *ontological question* about the nature of the person and the social system needed to sustain personal dignity, and the *epistemological question* of how we come to know the truth about the person and the human community.[2] These two methodological questions yield an ethical vision rooted in the concept of human dignity, but expand that concept to include a total theory of society. The move from a conviction about the unique dignity of the person to a conception of social order which will support and sustain human dignity is made in terms of a theory of human rights and duties. Personal dignity is both protected and promoted in terms of human rights. In Catholic theory, rights are moral claims which each person has solely in virtue of his/her basic human dignity; the claims are both inviolable and inalienable. Two kinds of moral claims exist. Some rights are immunities; they function as a protective shield insulating the person from unwarranted intrusion by other individuals, organized groups, or, most importantly, by the power of the state. Other rights are empowerments or positive claims which the person makes on others or on society as a whole in the name of basic human needs.[3]

In Catholic teaching, the theory of rights is linked to a correlative set of duties or responsibilities. Specifically, duties precede rights: Because I have a duty to preserve my life, I also have the right to those means necessary to fulfill this duty. Such means include minimal levels of food, clothing, housing, health care, and the crucial right to employment. Moreover, rights and duties are not only correlated within each person, they also are correlative claims among persons: If I have a right someone else has a duty to respect my right. This correlation of rights and duties in Catholic teaching sets it apart from the liberal philosophy which speaks of rights but seldom has an articulated theory of duties.

A second distinguishing mark of a natural law theory of human rights is its stress on the social nature of the person. The person is radically social; society precedes the person historically and the person is dependent on a social context for full human development. This strong social emphasis sets Catholic theory in tension with the more individualistic tenor of a social contract view of human rights. The importance given to society and social structure in natural law theory has produced an extended discussion of the nature of the state, its relationship to society, its role in the economy and its place in the international community. As one commentator has observed: "The placing of limits upon the arbitrary exercise of political or legislative power may well be said to have been the historical function of the doctrine of a natural law and, in fact, the thread of continuity linking its various forms in successive historical epochs."[4]

The natural law tradition on human rights therefore is part of a wider social ethic. Indeed, it is precisely in terms of an international perspective of human rights that the full range of the moral theory becomes clear.

The human rights argument is always linked to a conception of political order in domestic society as well as to some theory of world order in international life. It is possible to trace in Catholic thought and practice the successive forms of this human rights-political order argument. Aquinas' natural law theory is cast in terms of the Respublica Christiana of the medieval period; Vitoria contributed through his natural law view to the development of a theory of positive international law. Pius XII, in his Christmas addresses of the postwar period continually joined a natural law-human rights advocacy with a call for the political and legal ordering of the international community.

Finally in John XXIII's *Peace on Earth* (1963), we find the most fully articulated human rights argument in modern Catholic teaching. Charles Curran describes the encyclical as, "perhaps the most explicit affirmation of natural law as the basis of papal social teaching and the best illustration of its explication in social morality."[5] Although a detailed analysis of the encyclical is not possible here, I will simply point to it as the clearest exposition of a contemporary Catholic view of both natural law theory on human rights and the political order necessary to sustain human rights, from interpersonal relations through international relations.

Having said this, it is necessary to add a final comment about the status of a natural view of social ethics in contemporary Catholic theology. Precisely because *Peace on Earth* so explicitly states the natural law view of human rights, it is necessary to indicate the significant shift away from natural law argument in Catholic teaching which occurred just after its publication. The shift is represented in the Vatican II document the Pastoral Constitution on the Church in the Modern World (1965) published just two years after *Peace on Earth.* What one finds in the conciliar text is not a rejection of natural law but a move to incorporate its philosophical view of human rights in a much wider theological framework. There is in the Pastoral Constitution a more extensive use of Scripture, a more direct link drawn between Christology and social philosophy and a grounding of the human rights claims of the person in explicitly theological assertions.

This move to a more theological mode of discourse was due in part to the criticism which had arisen in Catholic theology that the understanding of natural law was divorced from our theological perspectives of sin and grace in history.[6] But it was also due in part to the dominant mood of the Council symbolized in the theological codeword, *Ressourcement,* a return to a more biblically oriented presentation of the faith. In the postconciliar period, the use of more explicitly biblical and theological categories in Catholic social teaching, including human rights, has been intensified.

To summarize the state of the question in Catholic social thought today, it is necessary to cite both the philosophical heritage exemplified by *Peace on Earth,* which in turn is rooted in the work of Aquinas and the social encyclicals, as well as the theological view exemplified in the Pastoral Constitution. The future relationship of these two trends is unclear; the theological mode of discourse is clearly dominant at the moment, reflected in one way in John Paul II's *Redeemer of Man,* as well as in other ways in the theological schools such as the Theology of Liberation.

The philosophical mode of discourse, however, is not only deeply rooted in Catholic thought, it also has an internal structure and a utility in a pluralistic world which cannot easily be replaced. Historically the Catholic tradition has attempted to blend faith and reason, theology and philosophy; it is unlikely that in the long run there will be any decisive break with this pattern, but it is easier for me today to illustrate the shifts which have occurred in recent years than it is to describe what form the dominant mode of human rights discourse will take in Catholic thought in the years ahead.

II. Catholic Ecclesiology and Human Rights

The shift from a principally philosophical to a theological statement of human rights is one point of methodological interest in Catholic thought. A second is the direct link drawn between the understanding of the Church's ministry and the pursuit of human rights. Ecclesiology is the branch of Catholic theology which systematically examines the nature and mission of the Church. Given the significance of these themes in Catholic life any major development in ecclesiology is bound to have a substantial impact on the presence and role of the Church in society. John XXIII's *Peace on Earth* was devoid of ecclesiological content; it was a superb piece of moral theory but there was no direct connection drawn between the moral teaching on human rights and the understanding of the Church's ministry and mission. The Pastoral Constitution of Vatican II, in contrast, ties the ministry of the Church to the pursuit of human rights.

In its central ecclesiological affirmation, the Pastoral Constitution describes the Church as a community of faith whose social role involves it directly in the promotion of human dignity and the protection of human rights. The conciliar statement describes the function of the Church in society as that of standing as the sign and safeguard of human dignity.[7] Since human dignity is intrinsically dependent upon human rights, the link between the Church and a human rights ministry is unmistakable in the document.

In the postconciliar period, both in theory and in practice, the bond between the religious work of the Church and the pursuit of human rights has been repeatedly affirmed. The 1974 Synod of Bishops in Rome issued a statement on "Human Rights and Reconciliation." Father Richard McCormick, analyzing the statement in *Theological Studies,* perceptively observed that the central text of the statement was neither its enumeration of rights nor its catalogue of violations today, but its ecclesiological affirmation that "in our day the church has grown increasingly conscious that the protection and promotion of human rights is central to her ministry."[8]

Both the moral theory and the ecclesiological reflection on human rights in the teaching of the universal Church have found expression in the ministry of the Church in the United States. This expression is not only the kind of practical involvement in questions ranging from the civil rights struggle of the 1960s to the role of human rights in foreign policy of the 1970s. It is also the fact that in explaining to its membership and the wider society what these issues of domestic and foreign policy signify in religious terms, the Church has used the language and the logic of human rights. The form of the statements reflects the more philosophical mode of argument of *Peace on Earth*, but the ecclesiological themes of the Pastoral Constitution are especially used to highlight the significance of the Church's work in pursuit of human rights.

Even though our attention in this essay is principally

focused on the United States, it would be a serious omission not to cite the way in which the human rights themes of both *Peace on Earth* and the Pastoral Constitution have provided resources for the Catholic community in other places. In the fifteen years since the Council, the Church has emerged in several countries as a principal adversary of authoritarian governments of the right and left which have successfully managed to silence, often ruthlessly, voices of protest and pluralism in the media, the universities, the labor unions, and the political parties. Often by a process of elimination, in cultures as diverse as Brazil, Poland, and South Korea, the Church is left as the single institution with some capacity to oppose by word and deed the arbitrary power of the state. It has not always been the case that the Church has responded adequately, but when it has risen to the challenge the justification for its action has been made in terms of human rights as a dimension of the ministry of the gospel.

It has been precisely the activity of some of these local churches which has helped us in the United States to examine how we are related by political policies, corporate practices, or treaty alliances to countries where human rights are being violated. The question for the Church in the United States has become what is a responsible posture for the Church here in light of what other churches are doing. This connection leads to the third consideration of my paper: the way in which the organizational structure of Roman Catholicism shapes our response to human rights question.

III. Catholic Polity and Human Rights

In assessing how the organizational structure of the Church influences our human rights work at the U.S. Catholic Conference, I would like to begin at a theoretical

level and work toward concrete examples. The methodological significance of establishing a rudimentary theoretical framework lies in the fact that the structure of
Roman Catholicism provides significant assistance in addressing human rights issues internationally. At the same
time, the structure also can make the implementation of
the policy more complex.

The question of protecting basic human rights in a
decentralized international system of sovereign states is
one of those issues which analysts of international politics today call a transnational problem. The emergence
of the category of transnational problems, including human rights but extending to other issues like population,
food, and resource policies, is one of the characteristics
of an interdependent international system. A correlative
characteristic is the emergence of transnational organizations. These are institutions which are based in one place,
present in several others, with a central guiding philosophy, a trained corps of personnel, and an extensive communications and control system. You will note this formal description of a transnational organization fits both
General Motors and the Roman Catholic Church equally
well.

The sociologist Ivan Vallier analyzed this transnational
character of Roman Catholicism in an essay which illuminates the potential of the Catholic organizational structure
far better than standard treatments of Vatican diplomacy
or Church history.[9] Traditionally the Church has functioned in the international system principally through the
Vatican diplomatic service, based in the Secretariat of
State, and present in close to a hundred countries, as
well as in all major international institutions, through
diplomatic representatives. This highly centralized mode
of international activity is the most visible form of Catholic presence in the international arena, but it does not
exhaust the presence.

Since Vatican II, the Holy See has mandated the creation of national episcopal conferences (like NCCB/USCC) in countries throughout the world. In addition it has encouraged the creation of "Justice and Peace" units in each country; these are charged with the task of mobilizing the conscience of the Church regarding issues of social concern, among which human rights is a preeminent question.

Finally, the religious congregations of men and women form an international network which has become both increasingly well organized and aggressively directed toward the social dimension of the Church's ministry. These international channels of action and communications reaching from the diplomatic curia to dioceses all over the world are the structures through which the Church functions as a transnational actor.

A fully developed analysis of this organizational pattern would have to examine the structure and function of each of these agencies, their interrelationships, and their impact on the fabric of international life. Such an analysis goes beyond the scope of this paper, but it is possible to indicate the dynamics of the transnational activity of the Church by examining three patterns of interaction: (1) the Holy See as the initiator; (2) the local Church as the initiator; and (3) interaction among local Churches.

The first pattern (Rome to the local Church) is presently exemplified in the Vatican policy of *Ostpolitik.* This diplomatic strategy, initiated by John XXIII and strongly affirmed by Paul VI, involves a delicate process of negotiation between the Holy See and governments in Eastern Europe centered on the human rights question of religious liberty. In this case, the local church is often too weak or fragmented to deal effectively with the government, so

the Holy See intervenes at another level in the name of
the local Church.

The second pattern (the local Church as principal agent)
occurs when the Church in a particular locality, addressing
human rights questions, either calls upon the Holy See or
other churches for assistance or provides for these other
actors a model of ministry on human rights questions. The
most visible example is the way in which the Brazilian
Church in particular, and most of the Latin American
Churches in general, have made the human rights issue
a priority for others (including the Holy See) in the Church.

Thirdly, since the formation of national episcopal conferences a pattern of interaction among local Churches is
emerging around human rights issues which involve two
countries. This decentralized pattern of interaction is a
noticeably different model than the classical diplomatic
pattern, but one well adapted to addressing specific human rights questions. This local Church interaction is often
aided by religious congregations working in the countries
involved.

It is the third pattern (local Church to local Church)
which we use most often at the U.S. Catholic Conference
on human rights. Three criteria govern our policy choices
of human rights cases. First, there must be an alleged pattern of human rights violations which we can document
with a reasonable degree of certitude. The process of documentation involves a mix of using government reports
(e.g., State Department Human Rights Reports), documentation of nongovernmental bodies (e.g., the International Commission of Jurists), and the testimony of the
local Church (either missionaries or citizens of the country).

Second, there must be some identifiable influence which
the U.S. yields in the situation. This criterion specifies one
aspect of our approach at the Catholic Conference. We see

most of our activity in terms of the Church in the United
States addressing the U.S. government about what constitutes a responsible policy in the face of human rights violations. U.S. influence can have multiple dimensions: military or economic assistance, political influence, trade relationships or treaties. Our basic policy approach is that
all these ties to other governments should be evaluated
in terms of human rights criteria.

Third, before we address a human rights question publicly, we need some indication of what the view of the
local Church is on the question. Specifically, as the Bishops Conference here we need some assessment of how
the hierarchy in the country concerned would receive
public action (e.g., congressional testimony) by the Church
in the United States.

In light of these criteria, let me identify three kinds of
cases which illustrate our involvement in human rights and
international policy. The first is U.S.–Latin American Relations (this includes several countries: Brazil, Chile, Nica-
ragua). In this case the rights violations are visible, systematic, and well documented. The local hierarchies are
for the most part aggressively committed with their priests,
people, and religious to a human rights ministry and they
welcome whatever we can do to influence U.S. policy,
governmental and corporate. This convergence of factors
has produced a sustained policy of human rights involvement for us regarding U.S.–Latin American relations.

The second illustrative case is Eastern Europe. Here
again human rights violations exist in a systematic pattern and are well documented. In this case, access to the
local hierarchy involves a difficult and delicate process of
communications; sometimes it is not possible (e.g., Albania).
Moreover, we must be consciously aware, in anything we
do as a local Church, of the larger pattern of activity involved in the *Ostpolitik*. Moreover, U.S. influence in these

cases is not through the same instrumentality (military and economic aid) as in Latin America. In Eastern Europe the relationships involve trade and a nuanced source of political influence. Consequently, the process both within the Church and with the U.S. government is more complex. We do address the human rights problem in Eastern Europe, but every decision takes prolonged consultation.

The third case is the U.S.–Philippines relationship. The pattern of human rights violations is systematic and well documented—often by Church sources. The U.S. influence is massive, but U.S. human rights interest has been less than systematic. The crucial problem for us on this question, however, is that the local hierarchy is divided about the kind of response which should be made to the human rights question. This division in turn makes the formulation of our response exceedingly difficult. We have responded, but with great care and not without some conflict.

Conclusion

From this matrix of moral theory, ecclesiology, and organizational policy, our response to human rights violations in international arenas is formulated. At all three levels there are "open questions" about our procedures. These are due in part to the complexity of the cases, but due also to the relatively new reality of the Church trying to take this question seriously as a central dimension of its ministry.

NOTES

1 C. Curran, *Catholic Moral Theology in Dialogue* (Notre Dame, Ind.: University of Notre Dame Press, 1976), pp. 117–118.

2. Ibid., p. 119.

3. John XXIII, *Peace on Earth* in J. Gremillion, ed., *The Gospel of Peace and Justice* (Maryknoll, N.Y.: Orbis Books, 1976), pp. 203–206.

4. B. Crowe, "The Pursuit of the Natural Law," *Irish Theological Quarterly* 54 (1977), p. 21.

5. C. Curran, p. 118.

6. Ibid., pp. 120–128.

7. Vatican II: Pastoral Constitution on the Church in the Modern World, in Gremillion, pp. 275, 312.

8. R. McCormick, "Moral Notes," *Theological Studies* 36 (1975).

9. I. Vallier, "The Roman Catholic Church as Transnational Actor," in R. Keohane and J. Nye, *Transnational Relations and World Politics* (Cambridge, Mass.: Harvard University Press, 1972).

Religion and International Human Rights: A Jewish Perspective

MICHAEL WYSCHOGROD

IT WAS IN JANUARY 1977 that a new administration was installed in Washington which made the issue of human rights central to its foreign policy stance. With the Vietnam War finally behind us and the foreign policy reign of Henry Kissinger ended, Jimmy Carter, first in his campaign and then in the opening months of his presidency, made it clear that human rights would play an important role in the foreign relations of the United States. In one sense, this could be viewed as no departure at all from the long-standing national consensus which saw America as a bastion of freedom and democracy, ideals in whose name the country had fought two World Wars. Still, the emphasis on human rights that Jimmy Carter brought to the White House in the early months of 1977 was widely perceived as a change from what had been accepted heretofore. Henry Kissinger, the previous Secretary of State, was not widely seen as a personality for whom moral considerations were paramount. He was interpreted as a twentieth-century Metternich whose notion of international affairs was rooted in the Congress of Vienna and the balance of power idea which succeeded in giving Europe a fairly long period of peace. Kissinger came across to the American people as a man of sardonic wit and sophistication. He seemed to know that nations were motivated by self-interest and that international catastrophes could best be averted by recognizing the various national self-interests and working within the parameters dictated by them. No one detected in Kissinger the vehement anticommunism of a John Foster Dulles, and this endeared him to the Russians, who seemed very comfortable with him. Serving at the helm of American foreign policy at a time of the greatest moral revulsion of American history—the ever intensifying moral protest of the American people at the Vietnam War—Kissinger succeeded in large measure in deflecting the moral revulsion from himself onto Richard Nixon, who was better cast for the role of villain. One can only speculate why Kissinger has drawn as little moral censure as he has. I suspect the real reason is that people perceive him as not vulnerable to moral self-condemnation and therefore relatively invulnerable to the moral censure of others. The world of Henry Kissinger is the world of power, in which the lesser of two evils easily becomes no evil at all.

With Jimmy Carter, a new wind seemed to be blowing. There was very littly irony in him. He was perceived as very American: religious, idealistic, and somewhat naive. His experience in government had not been in Washington and was nonexistent in the area of foreign affairs. In any case, we were suddenly presented with the thesis that respect for human rights was to become a cardinal principle of American foreign policy. We were not only to work for the realization of human rights in our country but we were to foster it everywhere in the world. This meant, in effect, that in our relations with other countries we would be concerned not only with the external actions of these countries but also with their internal policies. Regimes which violated the rights of their citizens

would have to realize that their relations with the U.S.
would be affected by their internal policies. America
stood for respect for human rights and Jimmy Carter
demonstrated this in various ways, not least of which
was a letter delivered to leaders of the Jewish emigra-
tion movement by the American embassy in Moscow.
The alarm of the Soviet authorities was considerable.
In fact, the first year of Carter's administration saw a
serious chilling of U.S.-U.S.S.R. relations, a chill which
began to thaw only after Carter eased up considerably
on his human rights rhetoric. Given the sense of illegitimacy under which the Soviet government labors, Carter's
human rights language sounded to the Soviets as a cal-
culated effort to foment unrest in the domain under
their authority, a prospect which undoubtedly panics
the Soviet governments in the extreme. It was difficult
for them to believe that Carter was not, in fact, setting
out to cause real dislocation in the Soviet world. It was
only as it gradually became clear that Carter was not engaged in a serious attempt to arouse those living under
Soviet domination to action against their oppressors,
that relations between the two superpowers gradually
improved.

But we must remember that the emphasis on human
rights which characterized the early period of the Carter
administration has all but disappeared. It is well known
that Henry Kissinger was critical of Carter's injection of
human rights into foreign policy from the beginning. It
cannot be said that this was based simply on a lack of
interest in human rights. In Kissinger's mind, the policies
of great nations cannot be modified by words and especially not by words directed at matters of internal
jurisdiction. For him, noninterference in the internal
affairs of other countries, particularly if they are powerful countries, is the norm that governs international

relations. The self-interest of the United States dictates that national power be brought to bear on those issues and in those areas of the world where important American interests are threatened. In his view, issues such as the successful conclusion of a SALT agreement or the restraining of Soviet influence in Africa and the Middle East are the proper concerns of American foreign policy. The injection of human rights talk into this context, from Kissinger's point of view, does little to advance human rights and much to retard solutions of the real problems facing American foreign relations.

We are thus addressing this question at a rather critical moment in the human rights in foreign policy debate. The fact is that, after a strong first act, the Kissinger view of things seems to have been vindicated. President Carter seems to have learned from experience that too much is at stake in the U.S.-U.S.S.R. relationship for him to correspond with Jewish emigrationists and other Soviet dissidents through the good offices of the American embassy in Moscow. Such gestures have ceased and we can ask ourselves what, if any, practical consequences have flowed from Carter's earlier emphasis on human rights. Was the initial Carter policy a misguided, naive attempt which was bound to fail, or has it, in fact, transformed the international climate? And, perhaps more germane to our concerns than any other, what attitude should religious bodies take to the question of human rights, particularly in respect to the place of human rights considerations in foreign policy decisions? Have we responded properly to the problems of human rights in Uganda and Cambodia, to take two outstanding illustrations of cases of serious violations of human rights in recent years?

It might be best to start with some scrutiny of the concept of human rights itself. On the abstract level, there should be little difficulty defining what we mean by human rights. The term refers to those inalienable rights which protect the human person in the exercise of his personhood as an autonomous moral agent whose rights to life and the free expression of his beliefs must not be abridged by political bodies. Our tendency in formulating a definition of human rights is to emphasize the dimension of political and religious freedom and to neglect the economic dimension. Marxist-oriented societies take exception to this tendency by insisting that political and religious freedom is a useful acquisition for those adequately fed and sheltered, but of very little use to those who are hungry and cold.

Right at the outset we thus face a fundamental clash between those who think of human rights primarily in political and religious terms and those who put economic well-being at the head of the list. It is an interesting fact that there is a general correlation between a society's political freedom and its level of economic prosperity. Economic underdevelopment is not frequently found together with a high level of political and religious freedom. Nevertheless, there is little reason to accept serious abridgment of political and religious rights in the name of economic development. The only way such a trade-off could be validated would be on the basis of the consent of those affected. It is an economically deprived population that would have to grant its consent to the abridgment of its political and religious freedoms and would have to reserve the right to withdraw that consent when it saw fit. The logic of the situation thus dictates, perhaps paradoxically, that only in a functioning democracy can political rights be curtailed justly for the sake of economic advantage and if such curtailment is to be revocable, the democracy of the political process must continue to function so that the electorate can, if it so wishes, withdraw its consent to the abridgment. Otherwise, the curtailment is imposed without the consent of the governed, and no amount of pleading of economic necessity can justify the imposing of curtailment of political and religious freedom by self-appointed dictatorships not based on the on-going consent of the governed.

Whether human rights are to be interpreted economically or politically is not the only problem that presents itself in the definition of human rights. Are there acts which are inherently wrong and constitute a deprivation of human rights no matter what the circumstances, or must any judgment that human rights have been illegitimately curtailed take into account the situation, the options available, and the consequences, real as well as anticipated, of various courses of conduct? Let me take the problem of torture as an example. There seems widespread agreement that torture of detainees is an infringement of human rights. It is worth noting that this was not always so. Throughout most of the Middle Ages torture was accepted as a legitimate means of ascertaining guilt, because it was believed that the innocent would never confess to false accusations, no matter how severe the torture. Confession, even under torture, was thought to be a reliable indication of guilt and therefore a legitimate tool of investigation. It may be that medieval man had a higher threshold of pain or a more sterling character such that mere pain could never make him admit to falsehood. Be that as it may, our contemporary moral sensibility does not accept torture as an acceptable method of interrogation, if for no other reason than that we refuse to lend credibility to confessions extracted under torture.

But the question of torture is not thereby exhausted. Let us imagine—and in today's world it does not take a very inventive imagination—that we are dealing with a terrorist gang that specializes in murderous attacks on civilians by placing concealed bombs in civilian buses, schools, stores, etc. Let us further imagine that an individual is apprehended who readily admits having placed such a bomb in a school or other location which is going to explode at a certain hour but our detainee is not prepared to reveal the location of the explosive. Under such circumstances, does morality dictate that the interrogators in the case restrict themselves to pleading for the necessary information, or may they use more determined methods—let us now not shrink from the word "torture"—to ascertain the location of the bomb which, undiscovered, will kill and maim many innocent victims? In short, is torture always wrong, or, under certain circumstances, may it be considered the lesser of two evils? Specifically with regard to torture, I do not think much attention has been given to this question.

I raise the question of torture only as an example of the difficulty of defining the "right" in human rights even in such relatively clear-cut situations as the question of torture. The problem becomes far more complicated when the human rights issue is raised in the context of international relations. Here we are faced with a variety of countries, many of whose human rights practices leave much to be desired. It would of course be possible to conduct a survey and assign to each country a grade in human rights. This, while possible, and to a degree achieved by Amnesty International, is, of course, not easy because it requires accurate information about what is happening in the prisons and interrogation centers of various countries. The countries in question take extraordinary measures to make the obtaining of such information very difficult. Furthermore, there are all the possibilities of differences of moral evaluation, as we have seen in the question of torture. But even if all these obstacles could be overcome and a human rights grade for countries based

on reliable informaton could be assigned, the problem
from the point of view of foreign policy would just begin.
The international system is based on a system of alliances
grouped around the two superpowers. As the strategic
world picture changes, various countries move from one
orbit to the other. For our purpose it is not necessary to
define precisely what the groupings are or, indeed, how
many of them there are. It is clear that, to take Iran as
an example, in late 1978 and early 1979 Iran moved from
one orbit to another. In such a system, it is inevitable
that we develop a greater tolerance for human rights violations on the parts of countries allied with us as against
those not so allied.

Given the political situation in a particular country, it
is not difficult to argue, and possibly even with some
validity, that the human rights violations of a particular
country constitute the lesser evil when compared to the
forces that would come to power were the present government displaced by the forces opposed to it. We must
therefore conclude that states are not impartial observers
of the worldwide human rights scene but active participants in the dynamics of an international political process in the context of which human rights violations, real
or imagined, are evaluated.

Furthermore, the human rights issue on the international level conflicts with the alleged sovereignty of states
and the right of noninterference in the domestic affairs
of states. Here we are dealing with a very fundamental
principle of international relations. Nowadays, the issue
of sovereignty is either misunderstood or ignored. There
is a fundamental difference between individuals and states.
Individual persons are citizens of states. This means that
they are residents. When the rights of a citizen are in-
fringed by a fellow citizen, the aggrieved citizen has a
government to which to turn from which he can demand

redress. His relationship to his fellow citizen who, in his opinion, has aggrieved him, is therefore a mediated one. From the political point of view, he does not stand in direct relationship to his fellow citizen, but his relationship or the relationship of both of them is to the state, which regulates their rights in accordance with its law. There are those who claim that individuals were sovereign only in the state of nature which preceded the social contract that founded the state. Once the state is founded, only it remains sovereign.

The state, as such, is not a member of a broader community to which it has ceded its sovereignty. Were that the case, we would be dealing with world government, a concept not frequently heard nowadays but one which some have long advocated but never realized. The charter of the United Nations does not in any way infringe on the sovereignty of its member states. The charter is a treaty in which states commit themselves to certain obligations. But it is important to point out that no treaty obligation really binds a sovereign state either *de facto* or *de jure*. No treaty obligation deprives a state of its sovereignty. Let us compare a treaty obligation of a sovereign state with a contractual obligation entered into by the citizen of a state. Because a citizen is subject to the laws of the state in which he resides, he cannot unilaterally abrogate a freely assumed contractual obligation. Were he to attempt to do so, the laws of the state would come into play to compel him to carry out his obligations or to penalize him for failing to carry them out. But a state, because it is sovereign, can abrogate a treaty whenever it wishes to do so. While, in one sense, by so doing such a state would violate the treaty, nevertheless, since the treaty itself is not embedded in a wider polity by whose sanctions the state can be brought to justice, the unilateral abrogation of a treaty by a state cannot be said to be illegal, since the very meaning of sovereignty is that the sovereign state is a law unto itself, precisely because it is sovereign. As such, sovereign states cannot be brought to justice because, from the philosophic-legal point of view, they are not subject to any jurisdiction outside of themselves. Whatever treaties a state signs, implicit in any such signing is the inherent right to withdraw any commitment so made.

It is only when we grasp this fundamental concept of sovereignty that the significance of the principle of non-interference in the domestic affairs of states becomes clear. However important it might be for me not to meddle in the affairs of my upstairs neighbor, the fact that he is not sovereign diminishes the weight of my interference in his affairs. While it may still be improper for me so to interfere, since the state does have the right to interfere, my interfering in his affairs does not, so to speak, violate a sovereign entity. But for one state to interfere in the domestic affairs of another state is to undermine the possibility of peaceful coexistence among sovereign states. Because they are sovereign and because there is no law (I exclude, of course, the natural law or the law of God) that is capable of mediating conflicts among states, the only hope for peace among states is a scrupulous determination on the part of sovereign states to respect the sovereignty of other such states by not violating their territory or otherwise meddling in their internal affairs.

It is in this context that the reluctance of most states to interfere in the affairs of fellow states must be seen. Even in cases where moral states become aware of violations of human rights in other, less moral states, there is great reluctance to violate the principle of noninterference in the domestic affairs of states. It is felt that the evil unleashed by permitting states to interfere in each other's affairs is so great and bound to have such devastating consequences for the cause of international peace, that non-interference in the affairs of states which violate even basic human rights is the lesser of two evils. It was this reasoning, I believe, that formed the thinking of those, such as Kissinger, who could not support the new Carter policy of stress on human rights in the foreign relations of the United States. These critics point to the decline, until recently, in the number of Jewish emigrants from the U.S.S.R., among other things, as evidence that great powers cannot be moved by external pressure to change domestic human rights policies.

To summarize, the expert foreign policy establishment is dedicated to the improvement of interstate relations, which is a project considered of the highest importance in the nuclear age. The injection of human rights issues into this machinery is seen by this establishment as misguided and naive, destined to achieve very little in the area of human rights and almost certain to interfere seriously with the smooth conduct of foreign relations.

While it is true that Jimmy Carter has modified his human rights rhetoric, it would be a mistake to believe that his original approach has had no impact on the international climate. There are those who believe that the upheaval in Iran would not have happened had not the world climate focused attention on the human rights issue. The Soviet attitude has remained hard, with most of those identified with the Helsinki monitoring group remaining in prison. Because the critics of the early Carter policy base their criticism to a large extent on the contention that injecting human rights issues into international relations will not help the cause of human rights, it would be most helpful to assess what the actual consequences of the early Carter stance have been. Unfortunately, the picture is too complex for a very convincing judgment on this point. The world community, particularly the religious community, must face up to the questions posed by the human rights issue. I will now attempt to look at this problem in the context of Jewish-Catholic relations, both on the world and national levels.

To do so, I think we must first raise the discussion to a somewhat higher level of honesty. I refer to the question of interest, since the beliefs of a group as to what constitutes its interests influence its point of view. It is customary for discussions dealing with questions of justice to adopt an impartial, noninterested stance. Issues are argued on their merits, with no reference to the intents of the parties concerned. Each side presents its case as if it had been drawn up by a disinterested observer. The fact that the conclusions each side arrives at happen to coincide with its interests is a lucky coincidence, nothing more. The fact that the opposite kind of coincidence, in which an individual or group comes to a conclusion which is against its interests, rarely if ever happens is another interesting coincidence.

The truth is, of course, that interests are taken into account, and moral decisions adopted have a relationship to interests as perceived. That is not to say at all that nothing else but interests determines policies. Genuine moral considerations also are taken into account, and in situations where the interests of a group conflict with the morality of its position, there may be a reduction of the vigor with which its position is advanced. The point is, however, that it is less than honest not to face the fact that groups do pay much attention to their interests. I would argue that taking interest into account is not in itself immoral, though a full elaboration of this thesis cannot be attempted here. The first proposal I present, therefore, is that we not hesitate to speak of our interests and that we learn to take each other's interests into account.

We must next take into account that there is an inherent

discrepancy between the Catholic Church and the Jewish people. The Church is a church, while the Jewish people is a people. The Catholic is a Catholic and an American, Frenchman, German, or Pole. How these two identities interact and what the implications of this interaction are on various levels and in various circumstances is, I am sure, a complex question. There have been wars in which Catholic nations have fought each other. It is clear that under such circumstances, the national identities of the participants, including even Church leadership, have taken at least temporary precedence over the religious. While Jews have, indeed, fought each other on various occasions in the past, current Jewish consciousness, I believe, finds such a conflict unthinkable. The tie among Jews would just seem too strong. In taking positions on human rights issues, Jews therefore inevitably take very much into account Jewish interests which, in the area of human rights, involve those instances where Jews have been or are being deprived of their human rights. To the extent that human rights issues arise in Israel in the context of allegations of mistreatment of Arabs, Jews react by stressing the very real security problems facing Israel, though undoubtedly remaining uneasy about the possibility of such mistreatment. Perhaps a church finds it easier to adopt a judging attitude toward a nation because the two are not fused. In any case, the difference between a church and a people, even of a religious people, ought not to be overlooked.

Having paid our full dues to the sober realism of the practitioners of international relations and having taken fully into account the complexity of situations of opposing evils—such as deprivation of human rights on the one hand and the breakdown of the principle of noninterference in the domestic affairs of other countries on the other—we must now ask ourselves where we will go from here. Is linkage legitimate? Should we make SALT II or trade concessions to the U.S.S.R. contingent on the improvement of the human rights situation in that country? How about our relations with South Africa? How about Uganda? For years, we had reason to believe that dreadful evils were being committed there. Should the U.S. have intervened? And how about Cambodia? There, too, one heard about terrible crimes and yet it was not until the Vietnamese intervened that the offending government fell. What should the attitude of the religious community be toward such events? Do we stick with the noninterference formula or do we, at times, advocate intervention without being ashamed to say so? Enmeshed with these questions is the deeper question as to how far religious communities are duty-bound to take stands on social and political issues. To stay away from such issues completely is to risk turning religion into a form of empty spirituality and cultic zealotry so sharply condemned by the prophets of Israel. To jump into every passing political issue with both arms swinging is to court the danger of transforming our personal political preferences into profound religious teaching. Whether the Westway ought or ought not to be built in Manhattan or whether a sales tax is to be preferred over a value-added tax cannot honestly be inferred from the moral teachings of Judaism and Christianity. And to some extent this is true even of the proposed SALT II agreement. Involved in the evaluation of that agreement there are many factual issues about which good Jews and good Christians can come to different conclusions. And yet the matter cannot be permitted to rest there.

Most social and political issues come in varying shades of gray. But not all do. From time to time, evils appear on the world scene which are in a class unto themselves. These are instances of large-scale, premeditated murder of large numbers of human beings in systematic ways.

Among cases of this abnormal evil, in our century, would be the extermination of the Armenians by Turks in World War I, the Soviet Gulag System, the Holocaust of World War II, and the recent regimes in Uganda and Cambodia. I do not mean to imply that these are the only cases that fit into this category—some others might be proposed. I ask you not to accept my examples as the only possible ones but to focus on the concept. The concept is that there is much evil in the world and that most evil, evil as it is, is not altogether abnormal evil. Ordinary evil is evil enough: crimes of private individuals against other individuals, the economic injustices of various societies, and the limits put on individual freedom. But then there appear evils which are qualitatively different from all other evils. The paradigmatic case is the Holocaust. When the religious community is faced with such evil, a wholly different procedure ought to come into play. Here we must become much less timid than we usually are. We must give up the prudential stance, the endless weighing of the consequences of alternate courses of conduct and the normally understandable habit of speaking by allusion and indirection, of not mentioning names, places, and times. In most instances such prudential weighing of possible positive and negative consequences is very much in order. But there are circumstances in which such weighing is no longer acceptable. We must speak in clear, specific, and unambiguous terms. Perhaps our standing among the professionals will decline. Perhaps we will be called naive and irrelevant. We will be called those things even if we never abandon our veneer of diplomatic sophistication. But we are, after all, not diplomats. We are representatives of faiths accountable only to God and our consciences. And if we remained silent during the various holocausts of this century, we stand condemned before God and our fellow man.

There are those who will argue that we must never lose sight of the consequences of our actions. Those who do so represent a certain pragmatic utilitarianism that has wide currency in the land. But there is also the view of Kant, who teaches that certain things are right no matter what their consequences and others wrong no matter what the consequences. For Kant, lying is wrong, no matter what the consequences, even if the continuation of the world depended on the telling of one lie. Now, Kant may be going too far. His ethics might be overly rigid, not taking account of the diverse ramifications of most actions. But does there not come a point when religious communities must speak and even act unequivocally, lest we drown spiritually under the calculations and qualifications of the diplomats for whom diplomacy as usual is the only absolute that must be respected under all circumstances.

If there is any validity in what I say, then we have to recognize a class of human rights violations such that the usual rules cease to apply. You may have noticed that I have not provided you with a very clear definition of this class of abnormal evil. I have not done so because I am not able to do so. Certainly, numbers of victims have something to do with it. So does the degree of cruelty involved. And there are other factors. But basically it comes down to recognizing one when you see one. I cannot define a beautiful woman but I do recognize one when I am fortunate enough to see one. In the negative mode, the same is true here. I am fairly certain that the five instances I have cited are examples of abnormal evil, though there may be others.

Since the task of identifying such cases is largely dependent on the obtaining of accurate and timely information, I would propose the establishment of a group whose task it would be to monitor moral problem areas of the world by all possible means. Such monitors would, of course, discover much evil that would not add up to what I have called abnormal evil. But when they draw the conclusion that they have come across an instance of *bona fide* abnormal evil, all hell would break loose. Our religious communities would speak clearly and prophetically. We would name names and identify places. We would stop playing diplomatic games. We would dispense with subtle, allusive formulations which could mean one of several things. We would speak in a way that would leave no possibility of misinterpretation. In the face of abnormal evil, abnormal responses are necessary.

One final word about the issue of noninterference in the internal affairs of countries which we have dealt with in the context of the sovereignty of states. Here, too, the distinction between normal and abnormal evil would play a decisive role. When dealing with normal evil, noninterference, at least in the military sense, ought to be the rule. But when the situation reaches the level of abnormal evil, this principle of noninterference cannot remain absolute. Even had Hitler Germany not attacked Poland but restricted itself to exterminating millions of its own people, the world should not have refrained from military intervention. In Uganda, in my opinion, the Tanzanians took upon themselves a task that should not have been theirs alone. We are commanded: "Do not stand by idly at the blood of your brother." (Leviticus 19:16). There comes a point when military intervention is justified and the religious community has a duty to speak clearly when that point is reached.

At this writing, the *New York Times* reports the testimony of Mr. Warren M. Christopher, Deputy Secretary of State, dealing with guidelines used by the Carter administration in applying its concern for human rights violations to the conduct of foreign policy. Mr Christopher testified before a committee of the House that wrote a foreign-aid amendment in 1976 which calls advancement of human rights "a principal goal of the foreign policy of the United States." The article reports:

> Mr. Christopher conceded that Washington used widely varying tactics, from private diplomatic exchanges to public criticism, to focus attention on human-rights abuses, depending on which approach seemed most likely to be effective.
>
> "Only compelling considerations of national security can justify providing security assistance to countries with very serious human-rights problems," he said, citing one guideline. "Even when these considerations require us to go forward with military sales to such a country, we still restrict sales to the police or others involved in human-rights abuses."
>
> Another Administration guideline, Mr. Christopher said, was that "economic assistance that directly benefits the needy is rarely disapproved, even to governments with poor human-rights records."
>
> The Deputy Secretary listed these other guidelines that help govern the decisions of the interagency Group on Human Rights and Foreign Assistance, which he heads:
>
> –The Administration attaches "fundamental importance" to three categories of internationally recognized human rights: personal, economic and political.
>
> –The most effective strategy for obtaining improvements is one that combines "the full range of diplomatic approaches" with a willingness to use foreign-aid programs as a lever.
>
> –Decisions to grant or deny aid are often made on the basis of trends in human-rights performances, rather than simply the overall condition of human rights.
>
> "It should be apparent from these five principles that we do not rigidly adopt the same approach to foreign-assistance decisions just because two countries

have a similar human-rights situation," Mr. Christopher said. (*New York Times,* May 3, 1979).

It is quite clear to me that Mr. Christopher's judicious tone applies to normal evil, the more or less common instances of human rights violations. Here the nonrigid, pragmatic attitude he expresses is without doubt the correct one. But it should be supplemented with a less judicious, far more determined stance when abnormal evil is detected.

V. Methodological Conclusions

Introduction

HAVING EXAMINED THE understanding of our two religious communities in three representative areas, the final papers move to the fundamental question of articulating and comparing the methodological systems implicit in each. The art of comparing religious traditions is often based on a shallow comprehension of one or another of the traditions. And it can easily degenerate into apology or even polemic. For any religion, as an expression of communal faith, can fully be grasped only from within.

The papers and the process of the symposium in which they were initially presented provided an unusually intense experience of "the other" for all participants. These final papers came at the end of an experience of true encounters which saw breakthroughs in insight and empathy achieved both by individuals and by the group as a whole. In the clarity and honesty of their self-revelations, they embody the highest reaches of true dialogue.

Rabbi Roth pinpoints four elements that are "essential determinants of method in any human venture." These are: the goal to be achieved, the assumptions that function to determine the selection of method, the criteria for judging the success of the method, and the manner in which the method takes into account existing circumstances which impinge upon it. Distinguishing between what he calls the "sociological" and the "moral" approaches to social policy, Roth goes on to show, concisely and critically, how each of these four elements are present in the formulation of Jewish social policy.

Father Pawlikowski's analysis of the "state of the art" of social ethics in Roman Catholicism surveys the critical theological issues which have shaped Catholic social enquiry since the time of St. Thomas Aquinas. In so doing he identifies a basic shift in social policy theory that emerged with the Second Vatican Council and an unresolved methodological tension that still prevails in Catholic thinking as a result of the differing perspectives on religious liberty and natural law that characterized the conciliar documents.

In his concluding section, Pawlikowski suggests eight areas of "possible contrasts" between the Catholic approach and the Jewish orientation in social ethics as he understands it. This section is particularly rich as a source of ideas for future exchanges between Catholics and Jews.

It is fitting to end on this note of looking to the future. On the immediate level we are directed to areas for further exchange, and perhaps shared endeavor. On the higher level we are directed to a time when discussion of social problems will no longer be necessary—except perhaps as a historical exercise.

Methodology and Social Policy: A Jewish Perspective

SOL ROTH

A FEW GENERAL REMARKS on the concept of method are appropriate at the start. This concept is generic, applicable equally to logic, mathematics, science, art, theology, and other areas of human experience. Some aspects of a specific method are characteristic of the discipline for which it was invented; others are general. The general elements find exemplification in the theological enterprise of formulating and implementing social policy as much as they do in the mathematical process of deducing theorems from axioms and the scientific procedure of verifying hypotheses about the universe on the basis of experimentation.

There are four elements that seem to be essential determinants of method in any human venture. The first and, I believe, the most important is the goal to be achieved. If we seek to extract meanings that may be hidden in a set of statements, the method of logical deduction is suitable. If we aim for knowledge of the empirical universe, observation and experimentation seem to be the appropriate means. The method chosen flows somehow from the end to be attained. Second, assumptions often play a crucial role in the selection of a method. One recalls, for example, the era of rationalism, when it was assumed that the mind could, out of its own contents, extract truths about the universe and when observation was regarded as a source of deception and error. Scientific method then differed from what it is today, a difference that was ultimately derived from diverse epistemological assumptions concerning the best approach to the acquisition of truth. To the extent that theology is not a domain accessible to empirical procedures, the role of assumption in the determination of its methodology may be considerable. Third, success in achieving the contemplated goal is a crucial factor in the validation of a proposed method. This is an obvious requirement. The very definition of method implies that it is an *instrument* for the realization of an objective: If that objective is not attained, the means intended to accomplish it can hardly be elevated to the status of method. Finally, a method must somehow take into account existing circumstances. I recall reading a description by a well-known artist of the methods he employed in his work, in which he declared that his brush stroke is determined not merely by his conception of the total painting he intends to produce but even more so by the concatenation of colors present at the moment he applies his brush to the canvas. In any case, it is evident that method must take into account the materials available at any given time and introduce procedures for manipulating them in a way that will bring the individual or society closer to the attainment of the designated objectives.

I

All four elements of method are present in the formulation and implementation of Jewish social policy. Of paramount importance is the goal to be achieved. The goal that Judaism projects as the highest good, the *summum bonum*, is the introduction of sanctity into human life—the life of the individual, the family, and the community. The concept of sanctity may of course be interpreted in a variety of ways. Some take it to apply primarily to certain rituals practiced by a religious community. It is interpreted, alternatively, as relevant only or primarily to principles of morality. There are those who denigrate ritual in comparison with moral conduct and believe that the sacred is to be found only in human relations when human behavior is guided and inspired by moral precepts. Even on this interpretation, however, there is a vast difference between reducing the sacred to the moral and elevating the moral to the sacred. If the sacred is, among other things, that which has its source in the divine will, then the identification of the moral and the sacred is a declaration that moral principle has a divine source. The moral accordingly undergoes an elevation. If, on the other hand, as Immanuel Kant suggested, the holy will is one whose actions are determined purely by practical reason in conformity to the categorical imperative, that is, the voice of conscience, there is a reduction of the sacred to the moral. For the saintly individual, according to this conception, does not respond to the will of God but to a moral conscience to which an atheist may equally respond and claim for himself an identical degree of sanctity.

From the Jewish vantage point, therefore, whether the holy is that which characterizes ritualistic procedures or moral principles or both, an essential feature of the sacred turns out to be its divine origin. The goal of the sacred, even when it is interpreted as a character of the moral, should then be construed in terms of the human response to the divine will.

Now, the view that the introduction of sanctity into human life is the goal of Jewish social policy implies that it is essential to create institutions in which the sense of the sacred can be communicated effectively—hence, the emphasis in Judaism on the enterprise of education. Education is a means and perhaps the best means for instilling a sense of the sacred in the human personality. The hope is that if the experience of the sacred is transmitted successfully, it will spill over into the larger community.

It is essential to add that the Jewish educational process, in its classic form, focuses on action rather than information. The cardinal category of the Jewish religion is not the principle but the precept, the *mitzvah*. Its thrust is not so much theoretical, that is, to teach what we shall believe, as it is practical, to exhibit what we must do in response to the will of God. The author of a great rabbinic work (*Sefer Hachinuch*) explains the reason for it.

> Know then that the human being is moulded in conformity to his actions, whether good or evil. If a thorough scoundrel whose early thoughts are entirely evil will arouse his spirit and will strive and engage constantly in the study of Torah and the performance of commandments, though not for the sake of Heaven, he will soon turn to the good and with the power of his deeds destroy the evil inclination. For the heart is drawn after deeds. (Twentieth commandment)

This discussion is crucial to the question of the formulation and implementation of social policy. Fundamentally, two approaches to the solution of social problems are possible. One is sociological. Society's social structure can be transformed in such a way that the impact of specific problems may be reduced or even eradicated. This might be done by the restructuring of old institutions or the introduction of new ones. The other is moral. Alternatively, the individual members of society, through a process of education, may undergo changes in character which could also lead to the same result. If, for example, society is afflicted by theft or greed, one may propose the abolition of private property. In the absence of the possibility of material possessions, one could not take title to that which belongs to another, i.e., one could not steal. Further, in such a social context, greed would not be a very useful sentiment. This would represent a sociological solution. Or, one may attempt to instill within the members of society a sense of honesty and generosity of spirit together with appreciation of the sacred dimension of these moral virtues. This is a moral solution. It focuses on change in individual character rather than on the transformation of institutions. Private property could then be preserved, but theft and greed would be severely diminished. The enterprise of education is indispensable to the second alternative, which, indeed, is central to Jewish social methodology. In fact, Judaism seeks to create a religio-ethical society through that form of education that stresses action.

One important consequence of Judaism's emphasis on the practical form of education is that the family becomes the crucial instrument in the process that leads to the cultivation of the sense of morality and the development of a commitment to the moral principles. The burden of education does not belong exclusively to the school. It must be carried by the family as well, which, in the Jewish view, must even assume the greater share.[1] The school will fulfill the purpose of the communication of knowledge and provide the explanation, even the justification, of principles. But the practice of precepts must be prompted and supervised in the home and by parents. Respect for parents, for example, cannot be assured by class discussion. It is necessary that children be taught to practice the precepts of conduct into which the principle of respect is translated and which have the capacity to instill the attitude of respect into the hearts of the young. Examples can be drawn from the Talmud and the Code of

Jewish Law (Shulchan Aruch). When children are trained to avoid sitting on a seat reserved for a parent, to refrain from contradicting parents, never to respond to a parent with abuse, they learn, in practice, that sense of reverence that constitutes respect for a parent. Similarly, if the charitable inclination is cultivated by *acts* of generosity, parents cannot leave it to the school to instill kindness and unselfishness into their children. They must themselves supervise their children in the performance of such acts. It is for this reason that the primary responsibility for teaching children the Torah was placed on the parent. Hence, the family, because it is the most effective means in the task of developing moral character among its members, is indispensable to the resolution of those social problems accessible to moral solution.

But Judaism, even while it adopts the moral approach, does not repudiate the sociological approach. Hence Jewish social policy requires that the Jewish community shall advocate, in society in general, the creation of voluntary institutions that will enhance the status of the sacred and the enactment of legislation by government that will permit the existence and growth of commitment to that which is sanctioned by the sacred. Judaism places a great deal of emphasis on the need to live in a community in which the patterns of public conduct enforce rather than negate moral and religious attitudes. Thus it is judged desirable to avoid a city where certain institutions are not available, for example, judicial and penal institutions for the purpose of enforcing the moral code, charitable agencies to assist those in need, a synagogue, a school, etc. (Sanhedrin 17b).

Judaism would even allow change and experimentation with social institutions whose existence is assumed and implicitly sanctioned in the Bible. In the religious kibbutzim in Israel, for example, principles of modern socialism have been appropriated and elevated into the realm of the sacred by relating them to the biblical principle of justice. Rabbis have defended this innovation on the grounds that, even while the principles of socialism are not imposed as obligations by biblical and rabbinic traditions—the system of capitalism is clearly sanctioned—they do nevertheless represent a fulfillment of the requirements of justice, Jewishly conceived. Judaism would then allow experimentation and innovation in social patterns and relations in order to get closer to the realization of the ideal of justice in society. It is clear that while Judaism may focus on the individual and his moral development, it also strives to bring into being the kind of social structure that will facilitate the fulfillment of those moral principles advocated and sanctioned by Him who is the Source of the sacred.

But Judaism takes a further step. Where it is not incompatible with the preservation of genuine religious pluralism in our country, it would endorse legislation that will have the effect of encouraging the creation and the growth of institutions devoted to the achievement of the sacred. The separation of church and state is a political, not a religious, principle. Indeed, within Judaism itself, the political and the religious are inseparable; the city of man is incorporated into the city of God. Notwithstanding, Judaism must always take into account the political climate in which it finds itself to assure the preservation of religious freedom. Further, there is a rabbinic precept which declares "the law of the land is the law" (Baba Kamma 113a). Where a state in which Jews live prescribes that its citizens shall conduct themselves according to certain rules and, further, where these rules do not prevent Jews from fulfilling their religious obligations, they are required to obey them.[2]

Hence, Jews seek to respond positively and constructively to the separation of the religious from the political in American life. It is sometimes necessary to do so, and in any case it is the law of the land. There is a problem, of course, with regard to the extent of such separation, but this is a political, not a religious, issue. Its solution must be undertaken, not by Judaism and in conformity to its religious requirements, but by American democracy and in harmony with its understanding of the meaning of its Constitution. Americans with religious commitments will, of course, share in the political debate. But however the problem may ultimately be resolved by Congress and the Supreme Court, the result will be acceptable to Judaism because it has adopted the rabbinic principle, "the law of the land is the law." In any event, when a proposed law or a new American institution holds promise of enhancing the domain of the sacred and where religious pluralism is not threatened by it, it will be judged deserving of support.

In addition, Judaism will urge social legislation that will contribute to the achievement of social aims that are endorsed by the sacred. Laws intended to ease the pain of those oppressed by inflation or suffering from a severe recession may be interpreted as consistent with the requirements of mercy or justice or both and, in any case, if enacted, would create social conditions in which these religious ideals would receive implementation. Judaism would advocate such procedures, sanction them as acceptable social policies and applaud their application to society.

II

In truth, the methodological principles discussed thus far flow not merely from the objectives that the methods to be chosen are intended to realize, but also from certain assumptions that Judaism makes with regard to the nature of man and society. This brings us to the second important general determinant of method, namely, the assumptions adopted.

The first Jewish postulate that deserves attention is that the human being has an almost unlimited potential for spiritual development. As Maimonides puts it "Every man has the capacity to be as righteous as Moses or, for that matter, as evil as Jeroboam."[3] Granted that this is the case, it will not do merely to manipulate social patterns, that is to restructure institutions in order to achieve intended social objectives. It is also important, via the school, the synagogue, and, above all, the family, to mould personalities whose moral commitments will ultimately be reflected in social relations. But further, in the Jewish view, it is even *more* important. Greater emphasis is placed by Judaism on the building of moral character than on the creation of new institutional forms. This may be inferred from the fact that Judaism's system of religion is formulated in terms of precepts of conduct addressed to the members of the community rather than in terms of the portrayal of ideals to be achieved or detailed accounts of desirable economic, social, and political institutions to be created. The emphasis upon ideals and institutions alone, at least in the social arena, could have led to the conclusion that the way to realize Judaism's social aims is by means of sociological transformation alone. Judaism's self-definition in terms of commandments means that even the realization of the social objective is ultimately dependent on the development of moral character. Hence, the *mitzvot* are also frequently enunciated in the singular. The commandments are directed at the individual human personality. Hence, too, the ends to be achieved through the practice of the commandments remain essentially tacit and unspoken. Judaism appears to have opted in favor of the formulation of a method, confident that if the right method is employed, the desired goal will ultimately be attained.

There is a second postulate of Jewish thought relevant to our theme. Patterns of individual behavior and social relations which conform to Judaism's requirements, though they are not motivated by religious commitments, are also of value. One rabbinic commentary, for example, declares "Would that were they to reject Me, they would at least observe my commandments" (Jerusalem Talmud, *Chagiga* I, 7). The rationale for this judgment is that *mitoch shelo lishma, buh lishma,* those who observe the commandments for ulterior motives may eventually cultivate genuine religious commitments. In any case, there is value in the adoption of the moral and social objectives of Jewish life on a nonreligious basis and the pursuance of them even without any recognition of the dimension of the sacred that attaches to them. There is much in Torah that could be chosen on utilitarian grounds alone as conducive to man's well-being and his happiness. It is Judaism's view that a choice for pragmatic reasons may ultimately lead to genuine commitment.

It may even be the case that Judaism regards certain social ideals as possessing inherent value independently of the fact that they may also be an expression of divine will. Thus, the rabbis taught that certain things should be done, not because they represent a characteristically religious response, but because of *darkei sholom*, they contribute to peace in the community. Social patterns that assure the ways of peace even in atheistic society are deserving of support. Peace and justice, an indispensable means to peace, possess intrinsic worth. They should be pursued for their own sake.

This conclusion suggests that, in Jewish thought, a

certain legitimacy attaches to the domain of the secular. (Note that, in this context, the "secular" is not to be construed as the rejection of the sacred but as the recognition of the existence of values independent of the sacred.) The very same social ends which are embraced by religion in response to the divine will may be sought independently on purely pragmatic grounds and because of considerations of utility. Those involved in the latter enterprise are not engaged with the sacred; their endeavors have value nevertheless. The secularly inspired objectives may well be achieved by the means of the sociological method, that is, the restructuring and creation of institutions.

It is for this reason that both king and judge—that is, a sovereign power operating on the basis of the causal nexus that natural and social processes reveal, as well as judicial interpreters of the divine will—were part of the biblically prescribed Jewish community. As one rabbinic commentator put it, while the judge sought to instill the divine element into human affairs, the sovereign was concerned with the production of social arrangements that would assure conformity of human conduct to social norms regardless of whether such conduct was prompted by religious commitments.[4]

III

There is a third determinant of method, namely, success. In a sense, it is the most important one because a method that does not lead to the intended objective hardly deserves to be entitled a method. Success is the touchstone of methodology. The crucial question, however, is, what are the criteria of success?

It may be argued that, in the religious arena, successful methodology produces desirable results in the transcendental domain; that is to say, an action in the realm of nature is to be viewed not merely in the category of a cause with empirical consequences in the form of effects but also as producing certain results in a more important spiritual domain in comparison with which that which happens here and now is relatively trivial. If this view were adopted, the success of religious methodology could be tested only by the extent to which the actions of men in society reflect religious prescriptions. Their social implications would not be material. While there are rabbinic interpreters of Judaism who direct attention to the spiritual nexus in which human actions are involved, the social consequences are, nevertheless, deemed to be of paramount importance. Indeed, assuring justice to those who are exploited, providing sustenance to the impoverished and healing to the sick are spiritual actions of the highest magnitude. Hence, the Jewish criterion for the success of the methodology aimed at social policy is essentially empirical and quantifiable.

That criterion has two elements. Success is measured by (a) the degree to which social institutions generate social patterns of conduct that embody moral values, and (b) the degree to which individuals are motivated to conduct themselves in accord with these moral principles that lead to social arrangements sanctioned by Judaism. The first element will not, by itself, suffice. There are occasions when institutional constraints and moral patterns are weak, inadequate, or altogether absent. The international political arena offers a perennial example. The United Nations and other international bodies are not very effective in preventing the perpetration of injustice by one nation upon another. There are societies where portions of its members are excluded from human compassion and the protection of the law. Such, for example, was the Jewish people under Nazi dominion. A blackout in an American city often has the effect of leaving individuals and their property at the mercy of criminal impulses. When institutional constrainst are removed, the social structure may break down, and violence, looting, and theft may become the order of the day—unless individual consciences are sufficiently developed morally to prevent it. This is the Jewish objective. Success of social policy, insofar as Judaism is concerned, must be measured, among other things, by the extent to which moral principles are integrated into human personality.

IV

The final determinant of method is the character of the present. Prevailing conditions often dictate the means that must be employed to accomplish a specific aim. This applies to both enterprises—the sociological and the moral.

In the nineteenth century, for example, when rugged individualism went almost unchallenged, the sociological method that could be utilized to provide every human being with a minimum of goods necessary for survival differed radically from that which could best be employed in the twentieth century, in which the goal of individual security is pursued by government-sponsored social programs. What had to be done by means of voluntary institutions supported by philanthropic endeavors in the earlier period can now be accomplished substantially by federal and state legislation. The methods of yesterday differ from those of today, as do the institutions of charity from those of government.

Now, while the task of formulating and implementing social policies intended to arrange social patterns so that their human consequences will coincide with moral ideals is less difficult today than it was in the past, the reverse is true with those social policies whose purpose it is to mold moral character. In an era in which religious and moral commitment is widespread, the task of communicating it is less difficult. It may even be accomplished by instruction because existing community forces encourage, support, and strengthen the moral and religious posture. In a secular and amoral society, on the other hand, the task is incredibly more difficult. The methods of instilling commitment in a social context in which, by virtue of prevalent social forces, such commitments, even where they are present, are constantly suffering erosion have not been adequately established. It may perhaps be accomplished by the building of communities, pockets of religious and moral life, in which moral character with the capacity to resist the winds of doctrine and the morally destructive attitudes available in the marketplace may be developed. But it is obvious that the task is enormous and the methods different.

V

The sociological approach to social policy is much more popular today than is the moral approach. There are several reasons for this. One of these is the rejection of religious values because of the climate of secularism in which we live and the repudiation of traditional moral norms because they do not find support in the universe of facts to the study of which science is dedicated. This circumstance renders the task of religion all the more difficult. But, insofar as Judaism is concerned, there is no adequate substitute for the moral approach to the formulation and implementation of social policy.

NOTES

1. I am not describing that which, in fact, prevails in Jewish life today. For even within the Jewish community, the process of education has become overwhelmingly intellectualistic; the enterprise is, therefore, assigned to the school. Families have largely abdicated their responsibilities in this area. Here I describe only the ideal, what ought to be the case.

2. There are several exceptions. The law itself must be perceived as just. There is a talmudic discussion (Baba Kamma 113a) about what happens when the law becomes arbitrary. It cannot then be considered the law of the land. According to Maimonides (*Compendium*, "Laws of Robbery and Lost Property," Chapter V, Par. 14) no law is acceptable as law unless it is universalized. Unless a law is applicable to every member of society, it is not an acceptable law.

Further, in the context of American democracy, we abide by the law of the land, even when, according to the law of the land, we engage in discussion, possibly even in civil disobedience, if we perceive a law as unfair.

3. *Compendium*, Book of Repentance V, 2.

4. *Derashot, R. Nissim B. Reuben Gerondi (RaN)*, Aryeh L. Feldman, ed. (Jerusalem: Shalem, 1973), Sermon II.

Method in Catholic Social Ethics: Some Observations in Light of the Jewish Tradition

JOHN T. PAWLIKOWSKI

IT SHOULD BE OBVIOUS to anyone acquainted with centuries-old religious traditions such as Catholicism that these traditions show significant variations in their approach to central issues. Ethics is no exception to this rule. Hence it is exceedingly difficult within a single essay to offer a fully honed picture of the methodologies employed by the Roman Church in dealing with social policy issues throughout the ages. I therefore have a limited goal in mind in this presentation: to explain some of the methodological bases in Catholic social ethics, with special concentration on those of our own century. This means that I shall not closely examine the views of individual Catholic ethicists, even though I fully recognize that a comprehensive description of Catholic methology would require such an analysis.

In keeping with the nature of this volume I will also attempt to suggest some comparisons and contrasts between the methologies of Judaism and Catholicism regarding social policy decision making. I am fully aware of the pitfalls surrounding such an effort at interreligious comparison. Often such attempts are marked by gross oversimplification. But, with my personal background in the

Catholic-Jewish dialogue and my research in the discipline of social ethics, I hope to provide at least some valid points for discussion in this regard.

Social Ethics in Pre-Twentieth-Century Catholicism

Any serious student of Catholicism will soon recognize that the theological vision of Thomas Aquinas shaped in a significant way the thought of the church on social questions. In the synthesis created by Aquinas the primary stress fell on the duties of a person to society rather than on the rights an individual could claim within any given social setting. The end result of the theory of society and social obligation espoused by Thomas was to link the individual person to other persons and to the social institutions of the state by duties which were not conceived as an integral part of the person, but rather were seen as a consequence of the social functions which a given individual fulfilled. In other words, the basis of social policy was to be located in an agreed-upon set of duties attached to the important institutions and functions of the state. A person serving in these offices automatically acquired a whole set of social responsibilities. O'Brien and Shannon in their volume *Renewing the Earth*, describe the medieval situation in these words:

> What held the society together was a theory of social obligation that sprang from the very nature of the society and was understood from a theological point of view as related to a hierarchically ordered universe ultimately ruled over by God. Consequently, Aquinas and other medieval philosophers and theologians did not have a theory of individual or social rights; they focused on the duties incumbent upon individuals

because of their social obligations. This clearly implied
that social obligations took priority over individual desires or wants. As a result, claims against society were
made in terms of clearly specified social responsibilities
that were proper to various roles within the society.[1]

This emphasis on social duties brought out by O'Brien
and Shannon as a cornerstone of medieval social thought
had the effect of maintaining organic unity within medieval
society. Fulfillment of particular responsibilities by each
member of the society assured the presence of domestic
peace. Thus the methodological basis for determining social
policy in part resided in the *a priori* assignment of duties
and responsibilities to each social function in a community.
In such a situation the only condition under which an individual could legitimately claim infringement of human
rights would be for the state to impede his/her performance
of defined societal duties. Only the eventual collapse of
medieval society would force Catholic theology to rethink
its approach to what determines the shape of social policy.

Another central aspect of medieval Catholic thought
that is pertinent to the question at hand was its understanding of the relationship between church and state. A unity
between the two in which the Church prevailed was the
stated ideal. There existed the firm conviction in the Church
that with its reservoir of revealed truth this arrangement
would guarantee total justice in all aspects of social life.
Not even the slightest suspicion is evident that the Church
itself could ever be an instrument of oppression. As long
as the church-state relationship had not attained its ideal
point, the Church and its theology stood over and above
the state in judgment to assure that its actions were in line
with the perceived will of God.

An important by-product of this church-state conception was the principle that "error had no rights." I think
we cannot overestimate the significance of this principle

in probing Catholic attitudes toward social policy. It colored the whole picture and in particular any policy connected with human rights questions. In this model for the ideal society, those outside the Catholic Church were, *in principle,* not entitled to political and civil rights because they lacked the true faith. *In principle* needs to be underlined because in practice we do find outstanding examples of Catholic leaders, both clerical and lay, who defended the rights of non-Catholics. But these exceptions should be seen for what they were—the result of personal sensitivity rather than official Catholic teaching.

In many cases where toleration was practiced in Catholic countries, the hope of eventually converting people to Roman Catholicism was a major motivating force behind this toleration. The attitude towards the Jewish community is a case in point. Generally speaking, those moments which witnessed some reprieve from the regular cycle of persecution and degradation were marked by intensive efforts at conversion of the Jews. These periods were sometimes followed by new bursts of anti-human rights activities against Jews when the proselytizing attempts proved a massive failure.

It is interesting to note a certain double standard in Catholic history relative to minority rights. While Catholicism had definite notions of superiority when it dominated in a particular state, it was not above claiming civil and political rights for itself in those geographic regions where it found itself a minority religion. In this claim it frequently appealed to the notion of natural law, which we shall discuss shortly. In the end, it usually tried to negotiate the best possible deal for itself with respect to religious and political freedoms.

This viewpoint, faith as the determinant of rights, continued to hold a place of dominance in official Roman Catholic teaching well into this century. It was only buried, after a bitter struggle, by the Second Vatican Council's Declaration on Religious Liberty.

The third key concept of medieval social thought was natural law. From a theological perspective, natural law has provided Catholic teaching with an answer to the question: Does there exist a source of ethical insight and knowledge for the Christian apart from scriptural revelation? Does the Catholic share a measure of ethical wisdom with all humankind because of the common humanity that is the birthright of all men and women? The natural law tradition in Catholicism placed a great stress on the goodness of all God's creation and the existence of moral insight apart from the explicit revelation of the Scriptures. But it did so through a rather artificial distinction between nature and supernature that the majority of Catholic ethicists find highly questionable in the light of contemporary understandings of the human person. It is important to underscore the point—especially in the light of frequent misperceptions of the Catholic natural law tradition on the part of non-Catholics—that a coherent philosophical/theological theory with a widely agreed-upon content of beliefs called the natural law has simply never seen the light of day. Father Charles Curran makes this point well:

> It is a gross oversimplification to refer to the natural law as a coherent philosophical system acknowledged by most thinkers. Although many philosophers have employed the term natural law, they do not mean the same thing by the term. There is a common ground morality which is shared by many men, but there is no one philosophical system with an agreed-upon ethical content. In general many could agree with the basic tenet of Thomistic natural law which identified natural law with right reason. However, many would disagree with the philosophical development

of that basic insight and with the ethical conclusions reached by some proponents of Thomistic morality.[2]

The other foundation stones for determining social policy in classical Catholic thought were scriptural revelation and authority. The latter included the teachings of the popes and church councils and in a special way the writings of the Fathers of the Church. I will not go into these at any length. Insofar as Scripture was used, the practice tended to be to select isolated texts without great regard for their contextual meaning. In the use of the other two fonts, natural law and authority, classical Catholicism and traditional Judaism are not that far apart in principle. The one major difference I would highlight is that the Jewish tradition frequently left greater space for minority views, at least in theory. Catholicism, on the other hand, tended to have a much more unitive view of moral truth and hence gave only one answer to a particular social problem. The implication clearly given was that any other response stood in contradiction to sound morality. Traditional Judaism, however, while not hesitant to express the preferred moral stance on an issue, more often left open the possibility of following another moral path on a particular question while retaining a clear conscience.

With regard to the general areas of moral methodology classical Catholicism and Judaism are much closer to one another than either is to classical Protestant doctrine. This is especially true with regard to the question of sound moral action on the part of a non-Catholic or a non-Jew. Both Catholics and Jews admitted the possibility that a person outside their respective traditions could act in a highly moral manner on many occasions. On a theoretical plane, this remains a much more difficult assertion for classical Protestantism with its strong belief that only the saving grace of Christ can enable basically sinful human nature to respond in an ethically responsible fashion.

As we look at the foundations for pre-modern Catholic social ethics, we see that most of them have been seriously undercut or are in the process of being questioned in their traditional formulations. The first to go was the social duties concept. It bit the dust with the disintegration of medieval civilization. The church-state ideal and the natural law tradition continued to hold sway into our own time. But they too, as we shall see later on in this presentation, have lost much of their former weight. The same must also be said for both the scriptural and authority dimensions. Neither is any longer able to operate in the usual sense as a result of modern biblical scholarship and the reforms initiated by the Second Vatican Council.

All this is to say that the whole methodological basis for determining social policy in Catholicism has experienced serious erosion in the twentieth century. The Roman Church is really confronting the task of building a substantially new base for its social policy decision making. No one should attempt to conceal this reality. The crisis of modern civilization is something that Catholicism has been seriously working through only in this century and, for the most part, only in the past several decades. It is a process that is far from over. I might add in this context that Catholics can learn a great deal from Judaism in this regard, since it underwent this crisis much earlier on.

Social Ethics in Modern Catholicism

Modernity, especially the Enlightenment with its creation of new pluralistic societies, posed a real dilemma for Catholic thought. On the one hand Catholics were not above appealing for protection under legislation developed in the new, democratic societies. Yet their theology had not freed itself from the belief that Catholic domination of the state constituted the ideal wherever possible or the conviction that human liberties were ultimately a corollary of faithful acceptance of the religious truth possessed by Catholicism.

The United States provided perhaps the most interesting example of the conflict between Catholic theory and practice in the Roman Church. While the Catholic immigrants to this land without doubt felt themselves to be part of an overwhelming Protestant ethos, their overall experience was assessed as positive. Even when they stood up in protest against aspects of Protestant America, they did so in the name of what they felt to be the fundamentals embodied in the American Constitution.

One example of an endorsement of the American ethos as healthy for Catholic belief and practice can be found in an address that James Cardinal Gibbons of Baltimore delivered in Rome in 1887:

> For myself as a citizen of the United States, without closing my eyes to our defects as a nation I proclaim, with a deep sense of pride and gratitude, and in this great capitol of Christendom, that I belong to a community where the civil government holds over us the aegis of its protection without interfering in the legitimate exercise of our sublime mission as ministers of the gospel of Jesus Christ.

For the great progress achieved by the American Church, Gibbons went on, "under God and the fostering care of the Holy See, we are indebted no small degree to the civil liberty we enjoy in our enlightened republic."[3]

In the light of affirmations such as the one by Cardinal Gibbons it is no accident that the primary challenge to the "error has no rights" theology in Catholicism came

from the United States. We shall return to this point sub-
sequently in this presentation. But it is crucial to note at
this point that America produced a deep-seated experience
of a national Catholic Church which would in turn open
the doors for a major alteration in a traditional theological
base for social policy at Vatican II. Thus the American
experience would assume worldwide implications.

Before looking more deeply at the debate over religious
liberty at the Second Vatican Council it would be well to
focus our attention for a moment on the European scene
at the turn of the century. Here the Catholic Church had
to confront the challenge of Marxism, in particular its
rather successful campaign to organize the working classes.
This challenge provoked the issuance of the first modern
social encyclical, *Rerum Novarum* by Pope Leo XIII in
1891. This in turn was followed, forty years later, by
Pius XI's *Quadragesimo Anno*.[4]

The publication of *Rerum Novarum* was in many respects a startling event, given the previous history of Catholicism and the personal background of Leo XIII. No
historical precedent existed in the Roman Church for
such a decree. And Pope Leo himself was allied with
conservative, aristocratic forces in Catholicism which
were trying everything imaginable to block the spirit
of the Enlightenment from in any way affecting its
theology or practice.

It is legitimate to ask, therefore, the motivation for
the strong defense of the rights of workers made by the
pope, a defense that paved the way for participation by
Catholics in unionizing efforts not only in Europe but
in North America as well. A close reading of the encyclical will show that on the theological level it does not
represent as much of a departure from traditional Catholic theology as is sometimes claimed. One receives the
distinct impression that the overriding concern of the

pope was not the human rights of the workers *per se,* but
the fear that they would be lost to the Catholic faith if
Marxist unions stood as the only viable option for their
frustrations. Thus, I believe we need to admit that the
encyclical's defense of the workers is really a by-product
of the classic Catholic concern for preservation of what
is looked upon as the one true faith. One honestly has
to wonder whether *Rerum Novarum* would have appeared
if Marxism had not proved the threat it did. While I do
not wish to downplay the ultimate impact that the encyclical produced, it did not represent a major theological departure for Catholicism with respect to the foundations for social policy.

Quadragesimo Anno by Pius XI does move somewhat
closer to the modern discussion of social questions, such
as the human rights of workers. But here there is likewise
a sense conveyed that the preservation of the Catholic
faith of the workers is the bottom line. Though the first
two major social encyclicals contain an appeal to the natural law tradition, besides placing a strong emphasis on
the interrelationship between the human personality and
property rights in particular, the impression remains that
these principles would never have been promulgated by
Catholicism if Marxism had not posed a strong threat to
traditional Catholic hegemony over the labor force.

The pontificate of Pius XII did not bring forth any
new formal social encyclicals. His Christmas sermons,
however, did provide much of the groundwork for the
encyclicals issued by John XXIII. Pius XII was of course
heavily involved with World War II. We can gain some
valuable insights into the papal attitude toward social
questions by examining Pius' handling of the Nazi attempt to exterminate the Jews. Historians and popular
writers have debated at length the morality or immo-
rality of the way the pope conducted himself during

this tragid period. Could he have done more? Could he have been more effective in saving Jewish lives if he had gone more public in his opposition to the Nazis? To some extent this issue may never be satisfactorily answered, though the release of further documentation may clarify the picture somewhat.[5]

Over and above a personal evaluation of Pius XII, it is important for any investigation of the Catholic tradition on social ethics to understand the theological framework that conditioned his mentality and guided his decision making during this critical phase of human history. In her volume *The Holocaust,* Professor Nora Levin offers an assessment that shows keen insight:

> In the years of fateful concern to European Jews, this institution [the Vatican] was entrusted to a man who undoubtedly believed he was being scrupulously neutral in his appraisal of world-shattering events but who, admittedly, believed that National Socialism was a lesser evil than Communism. In this context alone . . . how could Jews be viewed other than as unfortunate expendables? After all, it was the Nazis, not the Bolsheviks, who were destroying them.[6]

An evaluation of Pius that closely parallels that of Professor Levin can be found in the writings of the Catholic sociologist Gordan Zahn, one of the first Holocaust interpreters in the Catholic community. Zahn says that, in the last analysis, the fear of communism on the part of the Catholic leadership determined the basic policy decisions made during the Nazi era.[7]

The aspect of Pius XII's papacy that stands in need of further examination is his ecclesiology. From all appearances it was an eccesial vision which fundamentally interpreted the Church as the institution through which the principal components for human salvation—the Eucharist and the other sacraments—were made available to the human community. Since the continued existence of the Church commanded the highest position on the pope's priority list, he felt compelled to devote his principal energies to keeping the church alive, no matter what the eventual cost in non-Catholic lives. As one Vatican spokesperson in the period remarked, a concordat is possible with the Nazi government but never with Moscow.

Let me emphasize that this ecclesiology was not intentionally indifferent or hostile to the rights and very existence of non-Catholics. Rather it so envisioned the Church and its purpose for existence that in moments of crises, when hard decisions were required concerning the institution's survival, non-Catholics occupied no central role in the definition.

One cannot, I want to emphasize, ever underestimate the link existing between ecclesiological outlook and social policy for Roman Catholicism. The theological perspective of Pius XII clearly affected the kinds of policies he endorsed during the Nazi terror. And the ecclesiological questions that surfaced in the papacy of Pius XII are still with us today. They have not been completely settled. Until they are clarified, I am convinced that Catholic responses to social issues will depend largely on the sensitivity and experience of individual Catholic leaders rather than on a vision which sees justice for all men and women as an integral feature of basic Catholic ecclesiology. I shall return to this point later on.

Following World War II a significant interest began to grow in sectors of Roman Catholicism, especially in the United States, in the issue of religious freedom. Fathers Gustave Weigel and John Courtney Murray were chiefly responsible for stimulating this concern. In arguing the case for a firm commitment to religious liberty and church-state separation as an ideal for Catholic theology, they relied heavily on the primacy and dignity of human conscience. Their views were routinely attacked for several years, often with great vehemence, by theologians such as Msgr. Joseph Fenton, who maintained that the Catholic ideal of church-state union should be enforced wherever politically possible. The United States situation was an accommodation mandated by political necessity, not the ideal for Catholics, as Murray and Weigel would have it.

The movement given birth by Weigel and Murray eventually won the day at Vatican II, but not without considerable effort. The Declaration on Religious Liberty had to overcome any number of discouraging obstacles during the four years of the Council. At times it actually stood on the brink of permanent shelving because of the feeling by conciliar conservatives that it broke with Catholic truth in not affirming church-state unity as the ideal model. This document was often described as the Council's "American" schema. There is little doubt that it represented the most unique and singular contribution by the American Catholicism to the Council.[8]

As a compromise text which avoids any in-depth discussion of a theology for religious freedom, the conciliar Declaration on Religious Liberty has been described by John Courtney Murray himself as a document of very modest scope. He spoke of it in the following manner:

> It is concerned only with the juridico-social order and with the validity, in that order, of a human and civil right to the free exercise of religion. The right is founded on the dignity of the human person; its essential requirement is that man in society should be free from all constraint or hindrance, whether legal or extra-legal, in what concerns religious belief, worship, and practice, both private and public.[9]

Seen with the glasses of history the Vatican declaration,

in spite of its admitted shortcomings, represents a critical
turning point in the Roman Church. Msgr. Pietro Pavan,
who worked very closely with Father Murray on the text
of the final document, has termed it "a new position that
reveals itself as an intrinsic development in the socio-
political teachings of the Catholic church."[10] One clear
implication of the declaration is its endorsement of the
democratic "constitutional" state as the best political
system for the authentic preservation of religious freedom. There is a clear abandonment of the Catholic-
confessional state model, which had the strong allegiance
of most Catholic leaders prior to the Council. Pope John
XXIII's strong commitment to this new model in his encyclical *Pacem in Terris*,[11] released in 1963 while the debate at the Council on religious liberty was at a crucial
state, without doubt swung the tide in favor of the
schema. The new theology had secured papal approbation.

The Declaration on Religious Liberty must be seen as
a significant new milestone in Roman Catholicism's attempt to grapple with the complex realities of modern
civilization. The era when Catholicism could expect the
government and its socio-political institutions to serve in
the capacity of defender of the faith had ended. The
highest value that the secular, constitutional state is
called upon to protect and foster is the personal and
social value of the free, unimpeded exercise of religion.
As a result, and this must not escape our attention, the
declaration carries a significance for all social policy decision making on the part of the Roman Church, not
merely for the limited issue of religious liberty. As the
collapse of medieval society destroyed one of the theological bases of Catholic social status, so Vatican II undercut another traditional base. Father Murray speaks
of the extended meaning of the document in this vein:

Thus the Declaration assumes its primary theological significance: formally, it settles only the minor issue of religious freedom. In effect, it defines the church's basic contemporary view of the world—of human society, of its order of human law and of the functions of the all too human powers that govern it. Therefore, the Declaration not only completes the *Decree on Ecumenism,* it also lays down the premise, and sets the focus, of the church's concern with the secular world. . . .[12]

Murray also understands the declaration as invalidating the post-Reformation and nineteenth-century theory of civil tolerance. Within the conciliar document, in his view, there has been elaborated a new philosophy of society and state—one more transtemporal in its manner of conception and statement. The new philosophy is likewise less time conditioned and more differentiated. Four main structural elements undergird it. They are the four principles of truth, justice, love, and freedom. Murray adds:

The declaration of the human and civil right to the free exercise of religion is not only in harmony with, but also required by, these four principles. The foundation of the right is the truth of human dignity. The object of the right—freedom from coercion in religious matters—is the first debt due in justice to the human person. The final motive for respect of the right is a love and appreciation of the personal dignity of man.[13]

It is useful at this point to reaffirm the fact that the ideas on religious freedom advocated by theologians such as Murray became acceptable only because of the lived experience of the Church in the United States. Not until a major branch of the Catholic community had functioned for nearly two centuries in a religiously plural society and its leadership had to admire such a context was there any realistic hope that the traditional theological conception of church-state unity could be moderated. Here we have a clear instance of experience forcing the hand of theology.

In assessing credit for the new social justice emphasis in the contemporary Catholic Church the figure of Pope John XXIII also looms large. For Pope John dismantled, through his writings and, just as importantly, through the sheer force of his personality and style, the old "error has no right" theology. His support of the idea of religious liberty in *Pacem in Terris* was crucial in securing approval of the Religious Liberty document in the Council. And the loving fashion in which Pope John welcomed Protestant and Orthodox Christians, Jews and Marxists broke down old barriers more forcefully than a hundred resolutions. John himself, especially in *Pacem in Terris,* buttressed his arguments by appealing in large measure to the natural law tradition. In this methodology he stood in the same spirit as The Declaration on Religious Liberty.

When we shift our attention to the conciliar document on The Church in the Modern World (*Gaudium et Spes*), we are struck by the beginnings of a basic shift in focus on social policy. This is true with regard to both argumentation and content. For one thing this document emphasizes the question of cultural rights, something little discussed in previous Catholic teaching. One of its most famous and innovative sections deals with this issue. What was happening at Vatican II, of which this stress on cultural rights is illustrative, is the internationalization of the Roman Church. In the same way that the experiences of American Catholicism had been responsible for eroding traditional theological attitudes on church-state relations, so the experiences of Catholics in the Third World, entering the Catholic mainstream for the first time, were transforming the discussion on social justice. It was no longer possible to speak about issues such as human rights from a narrowly defined natural law tradition developed in the West nor restrict human rights questions to the religious and civil liberties area. The bishops and theologians from the emerging Churches were bringing new issues to the attention of the worldwide Catholic community. Poverty, political oppression, hunger, housing, and the like have assumed a new priority status. This non-Western influence has become even more evident in the documents emerging from the bishops' synods held in Rome during the past decade.

After a careful look at the documents of Vatican II, in particular the ones dealing with Church relationship with the modern world and with religious liberty, the presence of a still unresolved tension becomes increasingly apparent. From one perspective it may be rightly said that the statement on religious liberty once and for all closed the door on a long-standing tradition of resolving social policy questions within Catholicism. *Gaudium et Spes,* however, immediately unlocked a significantly new dimension. Apart from content, a methodological tension also exists between the documents. Religious liberty makes its appeal on the dignity of the individual and on the basis of the natural law tradition; the Pastoral Constitution on the Modern World virtually ignores the natural law tradition and shifts its focus away from concentration on the individual person towards stress on communal rights. Civil and religious liberties, while certainly not totally ignored, do not receive the prime attention.

Some further elaboration of the shift away from the natural law tradition in *Gaudium et Spes* is in order. The term is almost entirely absent from the document. This certainly must be called surprising, given the importance of the notion in the history of Catholic social ethics and the ringing reaffirmation of it by Pope John XXIII in

Pacem in Terris. And the omission is quite deliberate as Father Charles Curran sees it:

> *The Pastoral Constitution On The Church* marks a decisive turning point in the understanding of natural law and tries to integrate the natural law more fully into the whole schema of salvation history. Both in explicit words and in theory the document generally avoids understanding the natural as a relatively autonomous order unaffected by sin and grace. The first three chapters of Part One of the Constitution illustrate the newer methodological approach which tries to integrate the reality of the natural or the order of creation into the total Christian perspective.[14]

The pivotal paragraph ushering in Part Two of the Constitution introduces a new term into the vocabulary of Catholic social ethics in laying out its theological methodology for dealing with five practical policy areas: "To a consideration of these in the light of the Gospel and of *human experience,* the Council would now direct the attention of all."[15] For the authors of this document human experience is not simply a synonym for natural law. This is quite clear. The text rejects any sharp dichotomy between gospel and human experience of the kind traditionally postulated for the relationship between gospel and natural law. Human experience is not restricted merely to the realm of the natural. Moral insight merges from the totality of the cultural experience in which transcendent elements play a vital role. Extrinsic evidence also exists for claiming a decided shift on the part of the Council relative to natural law methodology. A high Vatican official, Msgr. Charles Moeller, who collaborated in the drafting of the Constitution, has confirmed the intent to move away in the document from the Roman Church's usual natural law argumentation. Speaking to a World

Council of Churches meeting in Geneva in 1966, he indicated that the term "natural law" was not employed out of ecumenical concern.[16]

One of the definite weaknesses of Vatican II as a whole was that the tension between the respective methodologies of the religious liberty and church in the modern world documents was never brought to the surface for extended discussion. Some bishops showed sensitivity relative to the conflict. While speaking and voting in favor of the religious liberty schema, they expressed concern about its somewhat exclusive emphasis on the individual person in isolation from society as a whole.

The tension over the natural law remains one of the principal issues of methodology in current Catholic social ethics. The natural law tradition certainly continues to garner its proponents. Some have tried to recast it, following the theological lines of people like Karl Rahner. Others like Father Charles Curran feel that present notions of history and sinfulness, coupled with new sociological data make the natural law tradition obsolete.[17] It too frequently has become a bulwark in support of the status quo in social relations. I would personally side with the latter position.

The period since the close of the Council has witnessed further development in Catholic social justice thinking. And most of the recent documents in their argumentation have proceeded along the path carved out by *Gaudium et Spes* rather than by the religious liberty document or the natural law tradition. Pope Paul VI's encyclical *Populorum Progressio* (On the Development of Peoples) is one example. It uses the term "natural law" on only one occasion. And that is a citation taken from Leo XIII. For Paul VI it is no longer adequate to ground a theology of social ethics in a supposed natural order which God has imprinted in the hearts of people and from which the concrete rules for a well-ordered, just society can be conveniently drawn. To indirectly emphasize this point, *Populorum Progressio* is the first official Roman document to cite the works of contemporary scholars in the socio-political field.

In his first encyclical, *Redemptor Hominis*,[18] Pope John Paul II does tend to bring back a focus on the individual person rather than community, reversing in some measure the orientation found in the documents since the Council. But it is only a matter of degree, not a total turnabout. Nonetheless, he does not ground his argumentation on the natural law tradition; in fact, his approach to the fundamental holiness inherent in all people would seem to implicitly reject the nature/supernature dualism at the heart of the natural law position. He does make at least one appeal to the decree on religious liberty, but does not really employ its methodology to any serious degree. John Paul's stance might be best characterized as faith-initiated and exhortatory for the acceptance and proclamation of the gospel, rather than a theological exposé of the bases for social policy.

An increasing number of regional and national documents have also appeared since the Council. They need to be taken into account in any discussion of methodology. In this line we can point to the Medellin and Puebla documents, the statement of a group of Appalachian bishops in the United States on land rights, and the strong document from the Southern African Bishops Conference, to name only a few.

In these documents one notices a clear preference for the needs and rights of the community over strictly individual needs and rights, though some attempt to strike a balance is usually maintained. Another area where a definite shift is perceptible is the ecclesiological. The U.S. Appalachian bishops' statement is one good illustration of this. The defense of the land rights of the local population, the vast majority of whom do not belong to the Roman Church, is proclaimed in the name of all the people. And two statements from the 1977 Southern African Bishops Conference document strike directly at this point.[19] In paragraph fifteen the bishops urge Catholics in their region

> to give practical expression to the conviction that the Church's mission including work for complete human liberation and to the teaching of "Evangelii Nuntiandi" [1974 Roman Synod decree] that evangelization includes transforming the concrete structures that oppress people; and in the light of this, to strive that the Church be seen in solidarity with all those who work for the promotion of human dignity and the legitimate aspirations of oppressed people . . .

And in paragraph eighteen Catholics are encouraged

> . . . to undertake development work less exclusively within the Catholic Church and to move towards the whole of society, showing there the power of the Spirit in union with other Christian Churches and in cooperation with local communities, so as not to further divide people on lines of church affiliation in ordinary citizen and political action but to promote harmony.

In many of the regional documents it is clear that non-Catholics are no longer merely to be tolerated in the eyes of Catholic social theology. There appears to be increasing recognition, though admittedly not always articulated in the clearest of theological language, that the fate of the Roman Church is somehow intrinsically tied up with the fate of non-Catholics. The Church cannot be truly itself without concern for injustice visited upon men and women anywhere in the world. This mood represents a definite break from the ecclesiology that commanded the allegiance of the Church under Pius XII when he was faced with the Jewish question. A more thorough elaboration of the new ecclesiology still awaits the hand of the theological master-craftsmen.

This concludes our brief overview of the basic principles that have conditioned Catholicism's approach to social policy decision making. As should be obvious from the analysis, the methodology has undergone substantial changes in the last several decades. The dominant new trends that have appeared are the emphasis on community needs and rights, the expansion of ecclesiological vision to include non-Catholics as an integral component, and the stress on the human experience of the believing community as a source of ethical norms and evaluations. The tension between the individual and the community and the final determination as to whether the natural law tradition will retain any significant role in Catholic social ethics still awaits further discussion. But there is little doubt that this century must be seen as a major turning point in the history of Catholic social ethics.

Some Contrasts with Judaism

To round out my presentation I would now like to suggest some possible contrasts between the Catholic approach to the basis for social policy and the Jewish orientation as I understand it. These are tentative suggestions for further discussion—nothing more. A comprehensive analysis would require a much more extensive study of the Jewish materials. This caveat aside, the following points have surfaced for me from reflections on the question. These points, let me hasten to add, are not stated in any sequence of importance.

(1) Both Judaism and Catholicism have recognized that in determining social policy questions from a religious perspective Scripture by itself is not a totally adequate resource. Both have acknowledged that extra-biblical sources are indispensable. A major difference, however, is that Judaism has generally allowed for the preservation of minority viewpoints on particular questions, whereas Catholicism has had the tendency to adhere to one and only one valid answer for a given issue.

Part of the reason for this lies in the differing approaches to history in the two communities. Judaism, much more historically orientated than Christianity, has at least tacitly recognized that the flow of history might eventually bring a minoirty viewpoint in a given age to the status of majority opinion at a later date. Catholicism, working out of a much more static worldview, has been much more committed as a result to the notion of moral absolutes that remain unchanging and unchangeable throughout the course of human history. This situation is being altered to some extent in present-day Catholicism as European political theology and Latin American liberation theology are forcing upon the Roman Church a much more profound awareness of the need to take history seriously as a component of any sound ethics methodology. Charles Curran has referred to this phenomenon as one of the most crucial developments in Catholic social ethics in several centuries.[20] This is an area where Catholicism stands to learn much from contact with the Jewish tradition.

(2) Both Judaism and Catholicism have admitted the ability of people outside their respective traditions to make sound moral decisions. On the Catholic side, the usual basis for this position was the natural law. Increasingly, as Catholic social ethics shifts away from the natural law position, the question will need to be rethought.

Insofar as any rethinking has taken place thus far, it has moved in the direction of acknowledging that other religious traditions are authentic sources of revelation and hence provide the non-Catholic with the basis for the possibility of sound moral action.

I have never examined the Jewish tradition in depth on this question. I am not sure that the Jewish tradition has in fact really grappled with the problem methodologically. If it has, or wants to, I would imagine that one source for development would be the tradition about the universal covenant with Noah, of which the Exodus covenant is a specification.

(3) Judaism and Catholicism both have to wrestle with the fact that in our time modern biblical scholarship and new approaches to the role of authority in religion have seriously eroded the Scripture/authority base for social policy formulation as we have known it in the past. In many ways the history of modern Judaism can be seen as a history of trying to grapple with this erosion. The reality has hit Roman Catholicism more recently, but with equal intensity. How can Scripture be utilized in the development of contemporary social ethics? What force do, what force ought, concrete social policy decisions made by religious leaders carry for their membership? These are questions that both contemporary Judaism and Roman Catholicism are struggling to answer.

(4) On the whole, we would have to say that the social ethical tradition of Roman Catholicism is much more expansive than that of Judaism. This is historically understandable. Jews have not often found themselves politically in a situation where they had any opportunity to shape social policy. As a result, it is natural that Jewish ethics tended to focus much more on personal and familial questions and on the issue of community survival. In a few pluralistic countries such as the United States where

Jews have had some input into national decision making, the Jewish contribution has usually resulted from a generalized commitment to the Jewish prophetic tradition, coupled with an equally strong allegiance to the principles of Western democratic liberalism.

I have not found in modern-day Judaism a great deal of analysis of social policy decision making from a specifically theological point of view. This is even true with respect to a figure like Rabbi Abraham Heschel, who in many ways epitomized Jewish social commitment in our era resulting from specifically religious motivation. There are exceptions, of course, to this picture, such as Reuven Kimelman's attempt to establish a religious base for non-violent social change in the talmudic tradition,[21] some explorations of how the Jewish religious tradition might relate to contemporary ecological questions,[22] and studies on the significance of the Holocaust of the kind undertaken by Irving Greenberg[23] and Richard Rubenstein.[24] But, by and large, there is no social ethics tradition in Judaism akin to that found in Roman Catholicism, as I see it.

Part of the reason for the above situation may admittedly be the fact that Judaism has never taken the strong interest in philosophical/speculative theology that has marked Catholicism. Whatever the reason, however, it is my personal view that this represents a shortcoming in the Jewish religious tradition that stands in need of correction. This is especially true in our day, now that Jews enjoy the sovereignty of a nation-state. There is need, from my perspective, for Jews, both in the Diaspora and in Israel, to develop a more sophisticated theological method for handling questions relative to political decision making in terms of war, use of nuclear weapons, sale of arms to repressive regimes, political allegiances with repressive regimes, the role of minorities in Zionist ideology, and so forth. While I am deeply sensitive to

the belief of someone like Emil Fackenheim that *the operating* principle for Jews today, in light of Auschwitz, is
survival, espeically survival of Israel, I must question
whether this is sufficient in any by itself. I am not for
a moment pretending that Catholicism has handled all
these issues with convincing thoroughness. But, nonetheless, I do feel this is an area in which Jews can learn
something from the tradition of Roman Catholicism.
Very much involved here will be the kinds of questions
connected with the expansion of the ecclesiological vision
in Catholicism about which I spoke earlier. Where does
Judaism theologically place the survival of non-Jews in
any authentic self-definition?

(5) One area that has been very important in recent
Catholic social ethics is the notion of social structural
sin, the notion that sin is not only to be located in the
individual person but also in the social-political institutions and patterns of society which can lead otherwise
moral people into unjust ways of relating to their neigh-
bors. Liberation theology has made this idea central to
its thought. It was also stressed in the Medellin documents and emerged as a core notion in the 1971 Synod
of Bishops document on social justice.[25] Again I find no
real parallel concern in contemporary Jewish social ethics,
even though I myself feel that it is possible to argue for
the existence of such a notion in the Pharisaic revolution
in Judaism.[26] Here is another area where I believe contact with Catholic social ethics thinking might provide
fertilization for Jewish thought.

(6) Insofar as "human experience" has emerged as a
significant methodological category in contemporary Catholic social ethics, there is a need to ask whether there
exists any parallel to this in Judaism and, if not, whether
present-day Jewish social ethics would want to introduce
such a category into its scheme of things. One complicating aspect is that in Roman Catholicism this category has

been added largely as a result of the new influence of non-Western churches. Given the fact that Judaism is being more and more confined geographically to the Western world, will this seriously affect the content and method of Jewish social ethics? Do the non-Western Jewish traditions, insofar as they have been preserved, have anything to offer here? This is something I, for one, would be interested in seeing Jewish scholars explore.

(7) We might profitably examine how both Judaism and Catholicism root their social justice traditions in a prayer basis. The connection between social ethics and prayer is one that is becoming much more important in recent Roman Catholic thinking. Thomas Merton raised it in an American context, and liberation theology has discussed it from a Third World perspective. From what I have studied on the question, ethics also has a strong basis in the prayer experience in the Jewish tradition.[27] This is another area that I feel we could explore together.

(8) The final point I would raise has to do with how Jews and Catholics view the role of religion in social decision making in a pluralistic society. In many ways both of our communities have historically been minorities in a supposedly secular, but in most respects actually Protestant, America. We have experienced some of the same new freedoms of this pluralistic society and, on occasion, the same rejections as well. We both have been committed to the concept of the separation of church and state, Jews perhaps even more strongly than Catholics. Yet the time has come for both our communities to rethink our traditional outlooks in this regard. This in fact is already beginning to happen, as I see it, with some of the participants in this conference being directly involved in the ongoing discussion. All of us, I assume, are deeply grateful for the positive contribution the church-state separation doctrine

has made to the quality of our life together in this land. But, as Father Robert Drinan asked in a presentation to 1975 American Academy of Religion Convention in Washington, has the price of separation not been the "over-privatization" of religion in American life? The time has come, I feel, for both faith communities to ask together what role we want religion and religious institutions to play in shaping the public values of our society. I think it is one of the most important questions we now face as a nation, even though reopening it represents a potential mine field. Obviously, what we decide on this question will greatly affect how each of us methodologically approaches social policy decision making.

For me, it is imperative that Catholicism, Judaism, and other religious traditions begin to join hands in meeting the current cultural crisis in the Western world. The peoples of the West are now experiencing, on a mass scale, an unprecedented degree of personal freedom—call it a Prometheus Unbound experience—which is leading to a rejection of imposed values, from religious sources or elsewhere. Yet there is a genuine search afoot for new values and a hunger for a new spirituality. In June 1977, Dr. Robert Muller of the United Nations, in addressing a conference on transcultural spirituality, sponsored at Petersham, Massachusetts, by the Vatican Secretariat for Non-Christians, said that "The world is on the threshold of a new period in history in which our understanding and experience of spirituality catches up with the rapid pace of technology."[28] To respond to this challenge organized Judaism and Catholicism will have to work together with others to shape the public and private values of the new society that is arising in our midst. I am convinced that all fundamental value reconstruction in the future will need to be done in an interreligious setting.

Thus what we have been doing during this conference takes on, for me, a significance far beyond the limited scope of improving Catholic-Jewish relations.

At the 1976 Eucharistic Congress in Philadelphia, Archbishop Helder Camara of Brazil quoted a proverb from his country which goes "when we dream alone it is only an illusion, but when we dream together it is the beginning of reality." Here at Notre Dame we have begun to dream together of the way our respective religious traditions might join together in the determination of sound and just social policy. If we continue on our path, perhaps someday soon we will see a new reality, that reality in which justice and peace will finally kiss.

NOTES

1. *Renewing the Earth*, (Garden City, N.Y.: Image Books, 1977), pp. 21–22.

2. "Social Ethics and Method in Moral Theology," *Continuum* 7 (Spring 1969): 59. Curran develops this in more detail in his contribution "Absolute Norms in Moral Theology," in Paul Ramsey and Gene Outka, eds., *Norm and Context in Christian Ethics* (New York: Scribner's, 1968).

3. As quoted in George G. Higgins' "Introduction" to Walter J. Burghardt, S.J., ed., *Religious Freedom: 1965 and 1975: A Symposium on a Historic Document*, Woodstock Studies 1 (New York: Paulist Press, 1977), p. 4.

4. Texts of *Rerum Novarum* and *Quadragesimo Anno* can be found in William Gleason, ed., *Seven Great Encyclicals* (Glen Rock, N.Y.: Paulist Press, 1963).

5. For further discussion of this question, see my monograph *The Challenge of the Holocaust for Christian Theology* (New York: Anti-Defamation League, 1978).

6. Nora Levin, *The Holocaust* (New York: Schocken Books, 1973), p. 693.

7. See "Catholic Resistance? A Yes and a No," in Franklin Littell and Hubert G. Locke, eds., *The German Church Struggle an and the Holocaust* (Detroit: Wayne State University Press, 1974).

8. For a detailed account of the development of the schema on religious liberty, see Thomas F. Stransky, ed., *Declaration on Religious Freedom of Vatican Council II* (New York: Paulist Press, 1974).

9. Ibid., p. 131.

10. Ibid., pp. 13–14.

11. Texts of the encyclicals of John XXIII and Paul VI and the Second Vatican Council documents on religious liberty and the church in the modern world can be found in Joseph Gremillion, ed., *The Gospel of Peace and Justice* (Maryknoll, N.Y.: Orbis Books, 1976) and in O'Brien and Shannon, *Renewing the Earth.* The latter also contains the statement from the U.S. Bishops in Appalachia.

12. Thomas F. Stransky, ed., *Declaration,* p. 139.

13. Ibid., pp. 147–148.

14. *Catholic Moral Theology in Dialogue* (Notre Dame, Ind.: Fides, 1972, rpt. University of Notre Dame Press, 1976), pp. 125–126.

15. See Paragraph #46.

16. See Charles Curran, *Catholic Moral Theology,* p. 128.

17. See Charles Curran, "Social Ethics and Method," pp. 58–62.

18. See *Origins* 8 (NC Documentary Service) (March 22, 1979): 627–644.

19. *Catholic Commitment on Social Justice,* Series Pastoral Action 9. (Pretoria: Southern African Catholic Bishops' Confernce, 1977).

20. See "Social Ethics and Method," pp. 60–61.

21. "Non-violence in the Talmud," *Judaism* 17 (Summer 1968): 316–334.

22. Eric C. Freudenstein, "Ecology and the Jewish Tradition," *Judaism* 19 (Fall 1970), and Monford Harris, "Ecology: A Convental Approach," *CCAR Journal* 23 (Summer 1976).

23. "Cloud of Smoke, Pillar of Fire: Judaism, Christianity and Modernity after the Holocaust," in Eva Fleischner, ed., *Auschwitz: Beginning of a New Era?* (New York: Harper & Row, 1978).

24. See *The Cunning of History* (New York: Harper & Row, 1978).

25. Patrick Kerans, *Sinful Social Structures* (New York: Paulist Press, 1974), and Peter Henroit, "Social Sin and Conversion: A Theology of the Church's Social Involvement," *Chicago Studies* 11 (Summer 1972).

26. See "On Renewing the Revolution of the Pharisees," *Cross Currents* 20 (Fall 1970): 415–434.

27. See Herbert Weiner, *Nine and a Half Mystics: The Kabbala Today* (New York: Holt, Rinehart and Winston, 1969), and Max

Kadushin, *Worship and Ethics: A Study in Rabbinic Judaism* (Evanston, Ill., Northwestern University Press, 1964).

28. As quoted in the *Newsletter* of the American Catholic Bishops' Committee for Ecumenical Interreligious Affairs, 7 (April 1978): 4.

Contributors

Rabbi Ben Zion Bokser
Forest Hills Jewish Center, New York

Rabbi Balfour Brickner
Director, Department of Interreligious Affairs
Union of American Hebrew Congregations

Dr. Eugene J. Fisher
Executive Secretary, Secretariat for Catholic-Jewish
Relations, National Conference of Catholic Bishops

Rev. J. Bryan Hehir
Associate Secretary, International Justice and Peace
U.S. Catholic Conference

Msgr. George G. Higgins
Secretary for Special Concerns
U.S. Catholic Conference

Msgr. Francis J. Lally
Secretary, Department of Social Development and
World Peace
U.S. Catholic Conference

Rev. John T. Pawlikowski, O.S.M.
Professor, Catholic Theological Union, Chicago

Rabbi Daniel F. Polish
Associate Executive Vice-President
Synagogue Council of America

Rabbi Sol Roth
Jewish Center of Atlantic Beach
Executive Committee, Rabbinical Council of America

Dr. Seymour Siegel
Professor of Theology
Jewish Theological Seminary, New York

Most Rev. J. Francis Stafford
Auxiliary Bishop of Baltimore

Dr. Michael Wyschogrod
Professor of Philosophy
Baruch College, New York